SoundPlay

SoundPlay

Understanding Music through Creative Movement

Leon H. Burton and Takeo Kudo

MENC: The National Association for Music Education

Music selections (1–47) on the *SoundPlay* CD
composed and performed by Takeo Kudo.
Copyright © 2000 by Takeo Kudo.
All rights reserved. Used by permission.

Contents

Introduction

The birth of a child is viewed by many as one of the most wondrous experiences of human existence. Even visiting a hospital to view a newborn child is an enjoyable outing for a family. It is sometimes difficult to realize that for several months before birth the fetus has been living and enjoying movement of the body in its fluid-world habitat.

A fetus one to two inches long and about twelve weeks old begins to squirm and jerk in the mother's womb. As Melvin Konner has said in his wonderful book *Childhood,* "The main business of life in the womb is motion." Small though the fetus may be, and so minute that it cannot even be felt by the mother, motion is underway and continues through birth.

By the fourth month of pregnancy the fetus may be sucking its thumb, and by the middle of the pregnancy it will kick. The five senses are functioning to some degree by the seventh month of pregnancy, and some pregnant mothers who attend concerts and movies have reported that their unborn children move in the womb in direct response to the music they hear. Movement intensifies, the child is born, and the child's movements become even larger as more space is available to explore.

Movement is one of the most important aspects of life outside the womb. It is a joy to all to observe the incessant energy of young children as they begin to express themselves through movement. They gradually learn to crawl, throw, clap their hands, walk, jump, and move in many different ways. As children grow older, their movements become more refined and even stylized. Playground and classroom learning activities involve children in a host of movements; their small and large muscle groups are being trained to perform intricate movements. In short, body movement becomes a major activity of life.

This book presents learning activities that use the resource of body movement to help young children grow in their understanding of music and related content areas. There is a natural relationship between music and body movement: they both occur in time. The body can be used to respond to musical sound with movement, an activity that helps young children become focused listeners to music. Children can understand many things about music by responding to what they hear with body movement. It is to this end that this book has been written.

Creativity and the Young Child

Young children have an innate curiosity about things in their environment—things they can see, feel, taste, smell, and hear. Their eyes will fix on an object, and often satisfaction is never fully realized until the object has been explored. They need to learn such things as how it feels, what sounds it makes, how it tastes. This natural curiosity becomes increasingly apparent in the form of creative imagination and expression as they gain more mobility and develop finer motor skills. In their minds, things in their environment can even become something other than what they are. Their world becomes filled with imaginary creatures; dramatic play can occupy extended periods of their time; they dress up and role-play doctor or cook to their own delight. When comparing the behavior and interests of young children with those of older children, we begin to understand why researchers concluded thirty years ago that creative imagination peaks in young children at about the age of four and one-half and then begins to decline.

A goal of today's education programs at any level should be to promote and broaden creative imagination and expression in children, teens, young adults, and older adults. Creative thinking has much to do with the quality of life. It can make life's activities far more interesting and eliminate the problem of dull, routine living day after day. Few in our world continue to develop creative thinking skills following childhood because of the constraints placed on learners by society in general, the workplace, and the schools. And probably few in our world do not understand the value that creative thinking can add to life.

Education plays a very important part in the development of creative potential. A person cannot create unless he or she has the *wherewithal* with which to create; hence, the importance of education in becoming a creative person. Creativity is a process of combining known factors (knowledge, understandings, skills) into new relationships to produce new results—a new product, a new way of thinking and perceiving, or a new way of performing. Education is therefore essential to our growth in wherewithal, which, when stimulated in the right kind of learning environment, can enlarge our potential for becoming more creative.

Some in our world develop their creative abilities as a result of personal interest and motivation without the aid of formal instruction. They discipline themselves to learn new techniques, explore alternatives, gather new information, imagine what could be, experiment with materials, and independently pursue hunches. Through their disciplined efforts they learn to create music, sculpt, write poetry, invent, design, and engage in other creative endeavors. The discoveries they make through their independent efforts provide them with more wherewithal, which they then use for new creative adventures.

Most people need formal instruction to grow in wherewithal and then encouragement and positive settings in which to use newly gained knowledge and skills in creative ways. Many children are not inspired at home or in school to think creatively, and when this is so in the early years, there are diminishing possibilities in later years for those who are not self-disciplined and who do not independently pursue creative activity.

A primary goal of this book is to spark the interest of young children in creative thinking and to provide developmentally appropriate challenges for using the wherewithal they learn in creative ways. Creative imagination should be nurtured and encouraged at every educational level. But with young children, we have an opportunity to provide the kind of guidance that will lead them into creative activity throughout their future years.

Conceptual Understanding in Music

The explanation of conceptual understanding in music that follows has been especially written for early childhood teachers. The development of concepts in music will involve far more than what is presented here, but the explanation will be appropriate for the level of development anticipated for young children.

A concept is a generalization (a larger idea) that consists of a host of related aspects (smaller ideas). An example of a concept in music is *melody.* A child could be introduced to melody as the tune we sing when we sing a song. Our conceptual understanding of melody is expanded as we recognize that tunes, or melodies, consist of a series of *pitches* organized into a singable and logical pattern. Higher and lower pitches are arranged in a pattern that can actually be drawn or graphed to show the shape of the melody, or its *contour.* Some melodies may have short, separated sounds (*staccato*); some may have smooth, connected sounds (*legato*). In all of the songs young children sing there will be a *tonic pitch,* a pitch around which the other pitches in the melody gravitate (sometimes called a *home tone*). For instance, "Twinkle, Twinkle, Little Star" begins and ends on the same pitch, the tonic pitch, but not all songs begin and end on a tonic pitch. As more and more of the aspects of melody are learned and recognized in musical sound, the concept of melody is expanded. This is conceptual understanding.

A second example of a concept in music is *tone,* or sound. All music consists of tones. Tones have four basic qualities: *pitch, loudness, timbre,* and *duration.* It is very important for young children to have many experiences that will engage them in focusing on these four qualities in the music they hear. Recognizing that there are higher and lower pitches, louder and softer sounds (loudness), sounds that have different qualities or timbres (man's voice, woman's voice, dog bark, cow moo), and sounds that are longer and shorter (duration) is basic to understanding music. Many activities in this book are designed to help children build recognition of these aspects of the concept tone.

Another example of a concept in music is *rhythm.* From the experiences children have with musical sound, they will begin to recognize that in most music there is a *beat.* Sometimes the beats of a song are faster, and sometimes they are slower (*tempo*). A song or recorded music may gradually speed up (*accelerando*), and sometimes gradually slow down (*ritardando*). As children learn to recognize these aspects in musical sound, the concept of rhythm will begin to expand; hence, conceptual understanding.

In the three examples above, you will notice that melody, tone, and rhythm are described only in terms of musical sound—the things *heard* in music. Conceptual understanding in music for young children is possible only to the degree that the aspects of concepts (generalizations) can be recognized and understood through what is heard. At a later stage of development, musical concepts can be understood by experienced musicians as they analyze written music and *hear* what is seen

with the inner ear. This is not an ability that young children can develop; young children can recognize conceptual ideas in music only through what they experience in sound. The primary aspects of music highlighted in this book are presented at the beginning of the group of lessons titled *Understanding Music through Creative Movement.* A summary of the concepts and aspects in the lessons is presented in the Index on page 105.

This book presents aspects of music as basic ideas that young children can experience in sound and for which they can use movement to show their recognition and understanding of what they have heard. A goal of the activities is to help young children use their energy and their incessant desire to move their bodies in creative ways in response to musical sound. As they learn to move in a variety of ways, they are developing wherewithal that they can use in creative ways in the future. As you guide them in their learning adventures, you are providing a good foundation for their future conceptual understanding in music.

As children advance in their conceptual understanding of music, they should be introduced to the terminology of music that can serve as a reference to musical experiences. For instance, a young child may describe a musical experience as "the music got slower" or "the music got faster and faster." These expressions describe their experiences exactly, but as children become more literate in music, they should be introduced to the terms *ritardando* and *accelerando.* Young children should be encouraged to describe a musical experience with whatever words they choose, but as their development of literacy progresses, they need to learn musical terms that will describe what they hear and that will serve as a reference for future musical experiences.

Aural Development

This book has several important purposes related to the education of young children. A purpose that needs to be addressed and supported by those who use the materials is the *aural development* of young children learning how to become focused listeners to music. Our world is bombarded with sound—so much sound that we could lose our sensitivity to quality sound and become far less focused as listeners; hence, the need to develop good listening skills in the younger years.

The activities in this book are all concerned with focused listening. This is promoted as children (a) listen and respond with movement to music that suggests different ways to move the body, (b) use movement to show recognition of the different aspects of music in what they hear, and (c) listen and assume roles to portray through movement different characters and events in the sound stories they hear. Their participation in these kinds of activities will result in improved listening skills. They will learn to become discriminating listeners as they recognize more and more the different aspects of musical sound and how they are used by the composer.

A long-range benefit children will realize from the activities is that music of lesser quality will no longer have the same appeal; they will begin to notice in some music the absence of aspects of music that give it good quality. As they grow in their conceptual awareness of music, they will become more focused as listeners.

The Music

The music included on the CD with this book has been composed especially for young children. All forty-seven selections include sounds produced by a "synthesizer," sound-producing equipment that approximates many sounds, such as musical instruments, we are accustomed to hearing. For instance, synthesized sounds described in the lessons as clarinet-like, trumpet-like, and flute-like will be heard on the CD. These sounds are sometimes very close to the sounds of the actual musical instruments. As children become older, it

is important for them to differentiate between the actual sounds of instruments and synthesized sounds.

Children should have many opportunities to experience the sounds of band and orchestral instruments, both live and in professionally recorded performances. The synthesized sounds heard in the music on the CD, however, can serve as a useful introduction to experiences in sound for young children.

The Lessons

All of the lessons in this book are designed primarily for children ages three to eight. Each lesson has as its core of study a musical selection especially composed for young children to stimulate their interest in moving to musical sound. These selections are provided on the CD that accompanies the book.

The lessons are organized into two groups. The first group, *Movements for Moving to Music,* has been designed to help young children learn to move their bodies in twenty different ways. They will already know how to do some of the movements. A goal is to help each child learn to name and do all twenty movements and to differentiate between them both visually and aurally. Children who expand their abilities to move in many ways will have a larger repertoire from which to draw when given opportunities to move creatively. The music is provided to suggest different ways to move, and it is important that each lesson be repeated several times for children's enjoyment. This will help them become more flexible in moving and will result in better coordination of their bodies with musical sound. There are fourteen lessons in this first group.

The second group, *Understanding Music through Creative Movement,* consists of thirty-three lessons. These involve children in the creative use of movements they have learned to show their recognition of the different aspects of music. Music is provided for dramatizing stories and thematic ideas told in sound, and in these lessons children will create movements to represent the sounds they hear. The selections provide children with a wide range of musical experiences that they will find enjoyable, challenging, and interesting.

The lessons are not sequential overall, but it is recommended that the first eleven lessons be used before moving on to other lessons. Lessons twelve to fourteen should be used as a summary of the first eleven. Then, lessons fifteen to forty-seven can be used in any order.

Lesson Content. Each lesson opens with a title, the primary anticipated outcome or skill children are likely to realize from their participation, and sometimes a photograph of a child or children engaged in the activity. The section titled "The Music" gives the length of the recording and the order of events in the music. For the group of fourteen lessons in *Movements for Moving to Music,* the second section is titled "Movement Focus." It gives specific movement skills children are expected to develop. For the group of thirty-three lessons in *Understanding Music through Creative Movement,* the second section is titled "Musical Understanding Focus." This lists understandings children will likely develop from their participation. The next section of each lesson, "Materials and Equipment," lists what will be needed to implement the lesson. And the main section of every lesson, titled "Activities," includes teaching suggestions for guiding children in attaining the goals of the lesson.

National and State Standards in Music

In an effort to achieve greater accountability in education and help teachers design learning experiences for children, standards for educational programs describing "what children should know and be able to do" in various subjects have been adopted in every state. Most state standards are modeled after the national standards developed by national professional education associations for the different subject areas. The K–4 national standards for music and the MENC PreK standards for music were developed by the Music Educators National Conference (now MENC—The National Association for Music Education) and published in *The School Music Program: A New Vision* in 1994. The K–4 standards were also published by MENC that year in *National Standards for Arts Education.* The PreK and K–4 standards are included at the end of this book. It is important for teachers of children to become familiar with the standards and to use them to help focus learning in music.

Each of the forty-seven lessons lists the MENC PreK music standards and the K–4 national music standards that relate to the learning activities. But by becoming familiar with all of the standards for the level at which you teach, you may find other ways to address the standards through the regular music program you are presenting to children and through activities you design to expand learning through use of the lessons in this book.

The use of standards is a way to ensure that all children will have continuity of educational experience as they move through the grades. It is also believed that the standards will contribute directly to providing a quality educational program for every learner in every school.

The Teacher's Homework

It is important that prior to using the activities in this book you have some understanding of all the materials the book includes, and more specifically, what the activities are intended to accomplish. This will provide you with a theory and teaching plan for guiding young children in understanding music through creative movement, and will help you become more aware of ways to stimulate creative imagination. The suggestions that follow for homework preparation are of a more general nature and apply to all of the activities.

- Arrange in advance of presenting activities to have adequate space for children to move freely.

- Obtain a CD player that will produce a good quality of sound.

- Make certain that an electrical outlet is accessible in the area to be used.

- Check a battery-operated CD player to learn if the batteries have sufficient power.

- Dress comfortably for movement activities.

- Develop a positive mind-set for moving your body freely to model movements, when necessary, for young children.

- Approach all activities with a goal of enjoying moving to music and communicating your joy to children.

- Practice finding selections with the CD, and learn how to reset the disk to find them again.

- Study an activity and internalize its procedures so you will not need to look at the book during the presentation of a movement activity.

- Ask children questions during and following the activity to help them focus on specific musical understandings.

- Constantly look for ways to encourage children to think creatively.

- Praise children's creative efforts and help them learn to appreciate and acknowledge positively the creative efforts of others.

- Invite parents of children to join your class in movement activities occasionally to encourage movement in the home.

The degree of preparation you do will relate directly to how successful your presentations will be. Prepare yourself to enjoy this domain of learning with your children.

Use of This Book with Other Curriculum Materials

You are encouraged to first build an overall understanding of the range and content of the activities in this book and then decide how the activities may best be woven into your teaching plans. The activities could be used to embellish curriculum materials currently in use and to supplement the materials and procedures you and others have designed.

Use of the activities will likely stimulate thought about other kinds of movement activities that could be used to enrich the movement/physical education element of your early education program. And moving in response to music could also stimulate the design of other music listening activities for children that will help them expand their understanding of music. Simple instruments could be used by children to play accompaniments to the recorded musical selections provided with the book.

A natural outcome from use of the activities would be to create brief musical events using simple sound-producing objects and to respond to the events through movement. In essence, a goal of this book is to stimulate the creative imagination of both teachers and children and encourage them to create new patterns of sounds and movements that will add a vital element to the existing program of activities. It is believed that the activities in this book will not be an intrusion on a curriculum program currently in use, but rather they will add a creative dimension and help to expand its present focus on creativity.

Movements for Moving to Music

The first group of fourteen lessons is designed to help children learn to do, name, and differentiate between twenty body movements. The goal is for children to build a repertoire of movements that they can later use in creative ways to respond to the music they will hear. The specific movements are run, walk, hop, twist, jump, shake, bend, reach, skip, stretch, trot, spin, sway, swing, stalk, collapse, slide, jerk, crawl, and leap. You could add to this list other movements that you believe are important to include. The activities in the lessons will give specific suggestions for differentiating between movements such as jump and hop, or swing and sway.

Running and Walking

The children use movement to differentiate between music for running and music for walking.

The Music  Track 1

Running and Walking (1:04 minutes). The music begins with four short signal sounds and then alternates between running and walking sections of music. The order is four short sounds, then music for running, walking, running, walking, running, walking.

Movement Focus

The children learn to (1) differentiate between running and walking and other movements they know, and (2) use running and walking movements in response to sections of music in the recording.

Activities

1. Ask several children to demonstrate how to walk slow, then walk fast.

2. Ask several other children to demonstrate how to run slow, then run fast.

3. Tap a drum to a slow beat and ask the children to try to walk (step) to the sounds of the drum taps.

4. Tap a drum to a faster beat and ask the children to try to run to the sounds of the drum taps.

5. Without describing the music, play the recording "Running and Walking" and invite the children to use running and walking movements to respond to what they hear.

6. For another hearing of the recording, suggest to the children that they walk fast or run to the faster sections, run slow or walk to the slower sections.

7. Provide time for the children to create their own running and walking dances both with and without the recording or drum taps.

Materials and Equipment

- CD player

- recording of No. 1, "Running and Walking"

- drum with mallet

Related National Standards

PreK Content Standard 3, Achievement Standard 3b, 3c
Content Standard 4, Achievement Standard 4b

K–4 Content Standard 6, Achievement Standard 6a, 6b, 6e

Hopping and Twisting

The children use movement to differentiate between music for hopping and music for twisting.

The Music Track 2

Hopping and Twisting (54 seconds). The music begins with four short signal sounds, and then alternates between hopping and twisting sections of music. The order is four short sounds, then music for hopping, twisting, hopping, twisting, hopping, twisting.

Movement Focus

The children learn to (1) do hopping and twisting movements, (2) differentiate between hopping and twisting and other movements they know, and (3) use hopping and twisting movements in response to the sections of music in the recording.

Activities

1. Ask the children to stand in one place and to jump when you say the word "jump." Both of their feet should leave the surface together as they jump. Ask them next to do three hops when you say the word "hop." Hops are traditionally done on one foot, unlike the hopping of rabbits and kangaroos, in which two feet move together.

2. Play a game of hopping and jumping, using verbal cues to help children distinguish between the two movements. Activities for jumping are included in the next lesson.

3. Demonstrate for the children how to twist. Stand in place, turn your head and body from side to side with your arms following the body movement. This should be done as a more deliberate and forceful movement than standing in place and gracefully swinging the arms to follow the body. Twisting has been described as *somewhere between* gently swinging from side to side and jerking from side to side.

4. Play a game by asking the children to respond with movement to your alternating verbal cues to hop and twist. Then ask them to watch and follow you as you do alternating hopping and twisting movements without using verbal cues.

5. Continue the game by giving other verbal cues for different kinds of movements they know, including hopping and twisting.

6. Without describing the music, play the recording "Hopping and Twisting" and ask the children to use only hopping and twisting movements to respond to what they hear. Explain that after they hear four short sounds, they should begin using a hopping or twisting movement. Guide them to discover through listening to the music when to hop and when to twist. Play the recording several times to provide sufficient experience in differentiating between the sections of music.

7. For another playing of the recording—or at another time—invite the children to create their own hopping and twisting dance, adding any other kinds of movements they choose to use.

Materials and Equipment

- CD player

- recording of No. 2, "Hopping and Twisting"

Related National Standards

PreK   Content Standard 3, Achievement Standard 3b, 3c
             Content Standard 4, Achievement Standard 4b

K–4   Content Standard 6, Achievement Standard 6b, 6e

Jumping and Shaking

The children use movement to differentiate between music for jumping and music for shaking.

The Music Track 3

Jumping and Shaking (58 seconds). The music begins with four short, tapping signal sounds, and then alternates between jumping and shaking sounds and more tapping sounds. The order is four tapping sounds, jumping sounds, three tapping sounds, shaking sounds, three tapping sounds, jumping sounds, three tapping sounds, shaking sounds.

Movement Focus

The children learn to (1) do jumping and shaking movements, (2) differentiate between jumping and shaking and other movements they know, and (3) use jumping and shaking movements in response to the music.

Activities

1. Ask the children to stand in one place and to jump when you say the word "jump." Both feet should leave the surface together as they jump. Ask them next to do three hops. Hops are traditionally done on one foot.

2. Play a game of hopping and jumping, using verbal cues to help the children distinguish between the two movements. Activities for hopping are included in the previous lesson.

3. Ask the children to stand in one place and begin shaking when you give the verbal cue to shake, and to stop when you give the cue. Model shaking only if needed.

4. Play a game by asking the children to respond with movement to your alternating verbal cues to jump and shake. Then ask them to watch and follow you as you do alternating jumping and shaking movements without using verbal cues.

5. Continue the game by giving other verbal cues for different kinds of movements they know, including jumping and shaking.

6. Play the recording "Jumping and Shaking." Explain that they will first hear four tapping sounds announcing that jumping and shaking music is about to begin. Guide them to discover through listening to the music when to jump or shake. Play the recording several times to provide sufficient experience in differentiating between the sections of music.

7. Invite the children to create their own dance using jumping, shaking, and other movements either with or without the recording.

Materials and Equipment

- CD player

- recording of No. 3, "Jumping and Shaking"

Related National Standards

PreK   Content Standard 3, Achievement Standard 3b, 3c
           Content Standard 4, Achievement Standard 4b

K–4   Content Standard 6, Achievement Standard 6b, 6e

Bending and Reaching

The children use movement to differentiate between music for bending and music for reaching.

The Music Track 4

Bending and Reaching (1 minute). The music begins with two short signal sounds, and then music that suggests gradually bending up and down is heard. Two short sounds are heard again, then music suggesting reaching up, and then music suggesting bending. The order is two short sounds, bending music, two short sounds, reaching music, bending music.

Movement Focus

The children learn to (1) do bending and reaching movements, (2) differentiate between bending and reaching and other movements they know, and (3) use bending and reaching movements in response to the sections of music in the recording.

Activities

1. Ask the children to watch and do what you do. Bend from the waist up and down slowly, and then do slower and faster bends.

2. Encourage the children to take turns showing how low they can bend in both standing and sitting positions.

3. Again ask the children to watch and do what you do. In a standing position, begin reaching higher and higher with arms extended and eventually standing on tiptoes.

4. Explain that when you say the word "bend," they are to continue bending until you say "reach." They then continue reaching until the next verbal cue. Alternate using the words "bend," "reach," and "stop" as they respond with movement to your verbal cues.

5. Play the recording "Bending and Reaching." Explain that they will first hear two short sounds, then music that suggests they should bend up and down. Guide the children to respond with movement to the sections of music as they are described above.

6. Invite the children either individually or in small groups to create bending and reaching dances and include other movements they choose.

Materials and Equipment

- CD player

- recording of No. 4, "Bending and Reaching"

Related National Standards

PreK   Content Standard 3, Achievement Standard 3b, 3c
             Content Standard 4, Achievement Standard 4b

K–4   Content Standard 6, Achievement Standard 6b, 6e

Skipping and Stretching

The children use movement to differentiate between music for skipping and music for stretching.

The Music Track 5

Skipping and Stretching (1:10 minutes). The music begins with four short signal sounds and then alternates between skipping and stretching sections. The order is four short sounds, skipping, two short sounds, stretching, two short sounds, skipping, two short sounds, stretching.

Movement Focus

The children learn to (1) do skipping and stretching movements, (2) differentiate between skipping and stretching and other movements they know, and (3) use skipping and stretching movements in response to the sections of music in the recording.

Activities

1. Ask one or more children to show how they can stretch their bodies. As necessary, model stretching by using your arms in slow, gradual reaching-up motions combined with your feet in a gradual tiptoe motion. The children will be inclined to stretch quickly rather than gradually.

2. Since skipping will likely be one of the most challenging movements for young children, you are encouraged to learn how to skip so you can model the movement. Demonstrate skipping for the children and ask them to imitate your movement. Accept the children's approximations of skipping.

3. Ask the children to play a game by skipping and stretching as you give the verbal cues to skip and stretch. Then ask them to watch and do what you do as you alternate skipping and stretching movements without verbal cues.

4. Continue the game by giving other verbal cues for different kinds of movements they know, including skipping and stretching.

5. Play the recording "Skipping and Stretching" and ask the children to listen and to stretch and skip when the movements are suggested by the music. For other hearings of the recording, model stretching and skipping to the music as necessary.

6. Invite the children one-by-one or in small groups to make up their own skip and stretch dance without the aid of verbal cues, music, or your modeling of the movements.

Materials and Equipment

- CD player

- recording of No. 5, "Skipping and Stretching"

Related National Standards

PreK   Content Standard 3, Achievement Standard 3b, 3c
            Content Standard 4, Achievement Standard 4b

K–4   Content Standard 6, Achievement Standard 6b, 6e

Trotting and Spinning

The children use movement to differentiate between music for trotting and music for spinning.

The Music  Track 6

Trotting and Spinning (1:09 minutes). The music begins with four short signal sounds and then alternates between trotting and spinning sections. The order is four short sounds, trotting, spinning, trotting, spinning.

Movement Focus

The children learn to (1) do trotting and spinning movements, (2) differentiate between trotting and spinning and other movements they know, and (3) use trotting and spinning movements in response to the sections of music in the recording.

Activities

1. Model trotting movements (sometimes referred to as pony trots) for the children. The knees should be lifted higher than in walking and running. Invite them to imitate your trotting movements.

2. Provide adequate space and an area free of furniture for a few children at a time to spin round and round. Model spinning as necessary. Limit the children's spins to three or four at one time since dizziness may occur.

3. Play a game by asking the children to respond with movement to your alternating verbal cues to trot and spin. Then ask them to watch and follow you as you alternate doing trotting and spinning movements without giving verbal cues.

4. Continue the game by giving other verbal cues for different kinds of movements they have learned, including trotting and spinning.

5. Play the recording "Trotting and Spinning" and invite the children to use trotting and spinning movements to respond to what they hear. Explain that after they hear four short sounds, they should begin using trotting and spinning movements. Guide them to discover through listening when they should trot or spin. Play the recording several times to provide sufficient experience in differentiating between the sections of music.

6. Invite the children one-by-one or in small groups to take turns making up a dance that includes trotting and spinning and other movements they have learned.

Materials and Equipment

- CD player

- recording of No. 6, "Trotting and Spinning"

Related National Standards

PreK   Content Standard 3, Achievement Standard 3b, 3c
            Content Standard 4, Achievement Standard 4b

K–4   Content Standard 6, Achievement Standard 6b, 6e

Swinging and Swaying

The children use movement to show recognition of music for swinging and swaying.

The Music  Track 7

Swinging and Swaying (1:10 minutes). Waltz music begins and continues throughout. Swinging or swaying movements could be used at any time.

Movement Focus

The children learn to (1) do swinging and swaying movements, (2) differentiate between swinging and swaying and other movements they know, and (3) use swinging and swaying movements in response to the music in the recording. There are many variations of swinging and swaying movements. The descriptions below may be altered to accommodate personal preferences.

Activities

1. Stand in one place and ask the children to watch and do what you do. With your feet stationary, gracefully twist your body back and forth from left to right with your arms swinging and following the movement of the body. Identify this movement as swinging. On each turn of the body say the word "swing" ("swing, swing, swing," etc.).

2. Ask the children to watch and do what you do. With your feet stationary and your arms hanging loosely by your sides, gracefully lean from left to right and on each lean say the word "sway" ("sway, sway, sway," etc.).

3. Again ask the children to watch and do what you do as you alternate swinging and swaying movements. Help them learn to differentiate between the two movements as described above or as altered by your preference.

4. Play the recording "Swinging and Swaying." Explain that they will hear waltz music. Model swinging and swaying to the beat of the music. Since the movements are similar, they could both be done at any time to the music. You or a student could lead the activity by alternating swinging and swaying movements as the others follow the leader.

5. Invite children individually or in small groups to create swinging and swaying dances either with or without the recorded music and include other movements they choose to use.

Materials and Equipment

- CD player

- recording of No. 7, "Swinging and Swaying"

Related National Standards

PreK   Content Standard 3, Achievement Standard 3b, 3c
                 Content Standard 4, Achievement Standard 4b

K–4   Content Standard 6, Achievement Standard 6b, 6e

Stalking and Collapsing

The children use movement to differentiate between music for stalking and music for collapsing.

The Music  Track 8

Stalking and Collapsing (58 seconds). The music begins with four strange sounds, which are followed by stalking and collapsing music. The order is four strange sounds, stalking music that grows in intensity, and then collapsing or tumbling music.

Movement Focus

The children learn to (1) do stalking and collapsing movements, (2) differentiate between stalking and collapsing and other movements they know, and (3) use stalking and collapsing movements in response to the sections of music in the recording.

Activities

1. Ask the children if they have ever watched a cat stalk and creep up slowly trying to catch a bird. If some children have had such an experience, suggest that they demonstrate what they have seen. Model the stalking movement as necessary for the children to understand it. Then have all the children (as cats) stalk an imaginary bird.

2. Use a small nylon scarf to illustrate the idea of falling slowly to the surface. A large, lightweight leaf could also be used. On a surface with mats or a carpet, ask the children to imitate the slow falling or collapsing movement of the scarf or leaf. They should freeze in position on the surface momentarily as they complete the collapse.

3. Play a game by asking the children to respond with movement to your alternating verbal cues to stalk and collapse. Then ask them to watch and follow you as you alternate stalking and collapsing movements without giving verbal cues.

4. Continue the game by giving other verbal cues for different kinds of movements they have learned, including stalking and collapsing.

5. Play the recording "Stalking and Collapsing" and ask the children to use stalking and collapsing movements to respond to what they hear. Explain that after they hear four strange sounds, they should begin using stalking and collapsing movements. Guide them to discover through listening when they should stalk or collapse. Play the recording several times to provide sufficient experience in differentiating between the sections of music.

6. Invite the children one-by-one or in small groups to take turns making up a dance that includes stalking and collapsing and other movements they have learned.

Materials and Equipment

■ CD player

■ recording of No. 8, "Stalking and Collapsing"

■ small nylon scarf or large, lightweight leaf

Related National Standards

PreK   Content Standard 3, Achievement Standard 3b, 3c
   Content Standard 4, Achievement Standard 4b
K–4 Content Standard 6, Achievement Standard 6b, 6e

Sliding and Jerking

The children use movement to differentiate between music for sliding and music for jerking.

The Music Track 9

Sliding and Jerking (1:02 minutes). The music begins with a short piano introduction. Then sliding and jerking sections of music are heard. The order is piano introduction, sliding, jerking, sliding, jerking, sliding, jerking.

Movement Focus

The children learn to (1) do sliding and jerking movements, (2) differentiate between sliding and jerking and other movements they know, and (3) use sliding and jerking movements in response to the sections of music in the recording.

Activities

1. Ask for volunteers to imitate a person roller skating or ice skating. Then ask the children to follow you and go for a *skate* around the room using sliding movements.

2. Stand in one position and slightly jerk your body in various ways. Continue jerking different body parts and eventually ask the children to join you in doing jerking movements.

3. Play a game by asking the children to "slide" and "jerk" in response to your alternating verbal cues. Then without giving verbal cues, ask them to watch you and do what you do as you alternate sliding and jerking movements.

4. Play the recording "Sliding and Jerking." Help the children learn to recognize the sliding section that begins right after the piano introduction. Then guide them to recognize the alternating sections of sliding and jerking music as they move in response to what they hear.

5. Invite the children either individually or in small groups to create a dance—with or without the recording—that includes sliding, jerking, and other movements they choose.

Materials and Equipment

- CD player

- recording of No. 9, "Sliding and Jerking"

Related National Standards

PreK   Content Standard 3, Achievement Standard 3b, 3c
            Content Standard 4, Achievement Standard 4b

K–4   Content Standard 6, Achievement Standard 6b, 6e

Crawling and Freezing

The children use movement to differentiate between music for crawling and music for freezing.

The Music  Track 10

Crawling and Freezing (1:01 minutes). The music begins with four high-pitched signal sounds and then alternates between crawling and freezing-in-position sections of music. The order is four signal sounds, crawling, long freezing sounds, crawling faster, long freezing sounds, crawling still faster, and then slowing down and stopping.

Movement Focus

The children learn to (1) freeze in position, (2) differentiate between crawling and freezing and other movements they know, and (3) use crawling and freezing in response to sections of music in the recording.

Activities

1. In a carpeted or other suitable area, invite the children to follow you as you model crawling forward, sideward, backward, and in a circular direction. Later ask the children to show other ways to crawl they might know.

2. Play a game by asking the children to follow your verbal cues for "crawl" and "freeze." When you give the cue to crawl, they should continue crawling until you say "freeze." At that time they should hold whatever position they are in until you again say "crawl" or end the game.

3. Ask the children to show how they can crawl slowly and gradually become faster, then crawl faster and gradually become slower.

4. Play the recording "Crawling and Freezing." Without explanation, ask the children to listen to the music and discover when they should crawl or freeze in position. Give the children several opportunities to respond to the sections of music in the recording.

5. Invite the children individually or in small groups to create a crawl and freeze dance and to include other movements they choose. Encourage originality and provide opportunities at other times to repeat the activity.

Materials and Equipment

- CD player

- recording of No. 10, "Crawling and Freezing"

Related National Standards

PreK   Content Standard 3, Achievement Standard 3b, 3c
        Content Standard 4, Achievement Standard 4b

K–4   Content Standard 6, Achievement Standard 6b, 6e

Leaping

The children use movement to show recognition of leaping music.

The Music Track 11

Leaping (1:02 minutes). The music begins with two tapping signal sounds and then alternates between running, leaping, and resting-in-place sounds. The order is two tapping sounds, running sounds that get louder, a signal to leap, and resting in place. This pattern occurs three times.

Movement Focus

The children learn to (1) do leaping movements, (2) differentiate between leaping, jumping, and hopping, and (3) run and leap in response to musical sounds.

Activities

1. Ask for volunteers to take turns demonstrating how to get a running start and then leap. Model leaping only as needed to help the children understand the movement.

2. Play a game of hopping, jumping, and leaping movements. Give verbal cues to signal when to hop, jump, or leap. Help the children learn to distinguish between the three movements.

3. Play the recording "Leaping." Explain that they will hear two tapping sounds and then sounds that get louder and lead to a signal to leap. Upon landing following the leap, they should stay in position until the next running music is heard. The running, leaping, and resting-in-place music is presented three times in the recording.

4. Invite the children to create their own dance using hopping, jumping, and leaping movements without the aid of music.

5. If appropriate, play a game to learn who can leap the greatest distance. Use a marker to show where the leaps are to begin. After a child leaps, measure and record the distance. Later decide who made the greatest leap.

Materials and Equipment

- CD player

- recording of No. 11, "Leaping"

Related National Standards

PreK   Content Standard 3, Achievement Standard 3b, 3c
             Content Standard 4, Achievement Standard 4b

K–4   Content Standard 6, Achievement Standard 6b, 6e

Moving Creatively 1

The children move creatively in response to walking, skipping, running, and trotting music.

The Music  Track 12

Moving Creatively 1 (1:15 minutes). The music begins with four tapping signal sounds and then presents sections that suggest four different ways to move. The order is four tapping sounds, walking, skipping, two short shaking sounds, running, one tapping sound, trotting, walking.

Movement Focus

The children have an opportunity to recall music they heard in the first ten lessons. They will (1) reinforce their ability to differentiate between walking, skipping, running, and trotting sections of music; and (2) move creatively to the music using movements of their choice.

Activities

1. Ask for volunteers to demonstrate four movements: walking, skipping, running, trotting.

2. Play a game by giving verbal signals in random order for walking, skipping, running, and trotting. The children should respond with appropriate movements upon hearing your verbal signals.

3. Explain that they will hear music from earlier lessons representing these four movements. As you play the recording "Moving Creatively 1," they should respond with movements they believe the music suggests. Provide assistance only as needed to help them recognize the order of the sections in the music: walking, skipping, running, trotting, walking. Especially lead them to discover a return (also known as *recurrence*) to walking in the last section.

4. Play the recording again at other times and invite the children to respond to the music with movements of their choice. The goal is for them to create their own dance to the music, using movements they believe will express what the music sounds like.

Materials and Equipment

- CD player

- recording of No. 12, "Moving Creatively 1"

Related National Standards

PreK   Content Standard 3, Achievement Standard 3b, 3c
Content Standard 4, Achievement Standard 4b

K–4   Content Standard 6, Achievement Standard 6a, 6b, 6e

Moving Creatively 2

The children move creatively in response to hopping, jumping, leaping, and jerking music.

The Music  Track 13

Moving Creatively 2 (1:13 minutes). The music begins with four trumpet-like sounds that ascend in pitch. Then sections that suggest five different ways to move are presented. The order is four trumpet-like sounds, hopping, jumping, three tapping sounds, running in preparation for and then doing a leap and resting in place afterward, then jerking.

Movement Focus

The children have an opportunity to recall music they heard in the first eleven lessons. They will (1) reinforce their ability to differentiate between hopping, jumping, leaping, and jerking sections of music; and (2) move creatively to the recording using movements of their choice.

Activities

1. Ask for volunteers to demonstrate four movements: hopping, jumping, leaping, jerking.

2. Play a game by giving verbal signals in random order for hopping, jumping, leaping, and jerking. The children should respond with appropriate movements upon hearing your verbal signals.

3. Explain that they will hear music from earlier lessons representing these four movements. As you play the recording "Moving Creatively 2," they should respond with movements they believe the music suggests. Provide assistance only as needed to help them recognize the order of the sections in the music: trumpet-like sounds, hopping, jumping, three tapping sounds, running and leaping and resting in place, jerking.

4. Play the recording again at other times and invite the children to respond to the music with movements of their choice. The goal is for them to create their own dance to the music, using movements they believe will express what the music sounds like.

Materials and Equipment

- CD player

- recording of No. 13, "Moving Creatively 2"

Related National Standards

PreK   Content Standard 3, Achievement Standard 3b, 3c
            Content Standard 4, Achievement Standard 4b

K–4   Content Standard 6, Achievement Standard 6a, 6b, 6e

Moving Creatively 3

The children move creatively to shaking, twisting,
sliding, bending, and stretching music.

The Music  Track 14

Moving Creatively 3 (1:21 minutes). The music begins with four tapping signal
sounds. Then sections that suggest five different ways to move are presented. The order is
four tapping sounds, shaking, twisting, sliding, bending, stretching.

Movement Focus

The children will (1) reinforce their ability to differentiate between shaking, twisting, sliding,
bending, and stretching sections of music; and (2) move creatively to the music using movements of their choice.

Activities

1. Ask for volunteers to demonstrate five movements: shaking, twisting, sliding, bending,
   and stretching.

2. Play a game by giving verbal signals in random order for shaking, twisting, sliding, bending, and stretching. The children should respond with appropriate movements upon hearing your verbal signals.

3. Explain that they will hear music from earlier lessons representing these five movements.
   As you play the recording "Moving Creatively 3," they should respond with movements
   they believe the music suggests. Provide assistance only as needed to help them recognize
   the order of the sections in the music: tapping sounds, shaking, twisting, sliding, bending,
   and stretching.

4. Play the recording again at other times and invite the children to respond to the music
   with movements of their choice. The goal is for them to create their own dance to the
   music, using movements they believe will express what the music sounds like.

Materials and Equipment

- CD player

- recording of No. 14, "Moving Creatively 3"

Related National Standards

PreK   Content Standard 3, Achievement Standard 3b, 3c
           Content Standard 4, Achievement Standard 4b

K–4   Content Standard 6, Achievement Standard 6a, 6b, 6e

Understanding Music through Creative Movement

The second group of thirty-three lessons is designed to guide children in using the body movements they have learned to respond creatively to musical sound. The experiences they will have in responding to musical sound through movement will contribute directly to their becoming discriminating listeners.

The thirty-three compositions in this group will provide children with a rich and wide variety of musical experiences. Children will sometimes assume the role of an imaginary character and dramatize a thematic idea. They also will use movement to show their recognition of aspects of musical sound. And at other times they will individually create dances that reflect the nature or style of the music they hear. Some of the aspects of musical sound they will be able to recognize that are highlighted in the lessons are:

- the beat of music
- prominent rhythm patterns
- different timbres (qualities of sound)
- pitch (higher and lower sounds)
- louder and softer sounds
- tempos (faster and slower music)
- sounds of different duration (longer and shorter sounds)
- music that gradually becomes faster (*accelerando*) and slower (*ritardando*)
- the general contour (up-and-down movement of pitches) or shape of music
- short, separated sounds (*staccato*), and smooth, connected sounds (*legato*)
- music that includes an accompaniment (background of sound to a melody)
- a sequence of musical events (sections in music that result in repetition, contrast, and recurrence)
- music that includes only one kind of sound, and music that includes more than one kind of sound (simultaneous tones)
- music that gravitates around a home tone (tonic pitch) and music that does not have a home tone

High-Step March

The children high-step march and move their body parts to the beat of the music.

The Music Track 15

High-Step March (1:12 minutes). Brief drum-like sounds are heard first to signal that the music will soon begin. The music begins, and it has a steady, march-like beat throughout.

Musical Understanding Focus

Guide the children to focus on the following understandings as they listen to "High-Step March."

- Music can have a steady, unchanging *beat*.

- Movements can be made in response to visual cues.

- Instruments can be played "in time" with the beat of music.

- Movement can be used to show recognition of a steady beat.

Activities

1. Clap your hands to a steady beat and have the children stand and march "in place" to your hand-clap sounds. Encourage stepping exactly to the beat. Gradually ask them to raise their legs higher (high-step) as they march in place.

2. Have the children now clap their hands to the beat as they high-step in place. Help them achieve coordination of stepping while clapping.

3. Form the children into one continuous line. You be the leader at the head of the line. Have the children follow you in a march around the area as you clap your hands to a steady beat. Later ask them to imitate your clapping while following you and stepping to the beat.

4. Play a thirty-second section of "High-Step March" and ask the children to listen for the drum-like sounds and the music that follows.

5. Form the children into a single line for another march that you will lead. Stand in place during the drum-like sounds, and then begin marching in a forward direction to the beat as the music begins.

6. Eventually lead a march to the music that includes a variety of hand-clapping positions while marching in a forward direction (clapping up high in front of the body, below the waist in front, on the left side, on the right side, switching back and forth from right to left sides, behind the back, etc.). Change clapping positions every twenty seconds or so in a "follow the leader" march game. You may eventually let the children take turns being the leader, creating arm movements that the others will imitate.

7. For another playing of the march, let the children take turns, in groups of six, tapping rhythm sticks to the beat of the music while high-step marching.

Materials and Equipment

- CD player

- recording of No. 15, "High-Step March"

- pairs of rhythm sticks

Related National Standards

PreK   Content Standard 1, Achievement Standard 1d
        Content Standard 2, Achievement Standard 2b
        Content Standard 3, Achievement Standard 3b, 3c
        Content Standard 4, Achievement Standard 4b

K–4   Content Standard 6, Achievement Standard 6b, 6e

Tempo Game

The children move creatively to show recognition of faster and slower music.

The Music  Track 16

Tempo Game (1:12 minutes). Three tapping signal sounds are heard. The music, played by a trumpet-like sound, begins slow and gradually becomes faster; after a brief pause, the music, this time played by more trumpet-like sounds, again begins slow and becomes faster; after another brief pause, the music—this time played by many brass-like instrument sounds—begins fast and gradually becomes slower.

Musical Understanding Focus

Guide the children to focus on the following understandings as they listen to "Tempo Game."

- Music can gradually become faster (*accelerando*).

- Music can gradually become slower (*ritardando*).

- Music can change in tempo (slow to faster, fast to slower).

- Movement can be used to show recognition of music that becomes faster and slower.

Activities

1. Discuss with children how automobiles, airplanes, trains, and other forms of transportation have locomotion systems that require beginning slowly and gradually becoming faster, and how the reverse condition is necessary for stopping. Have a few children move creatively to demonstrate moving slow and gradually becoming faster, then moving fast and gradually becoming slower.

2. Tap a drum to produce sounds that start fast and gradually become slower. The children should listen and tell whether the sounds began fast or slow. Follow the same procedure tapping slow and gradually becoming faster.

3. Sing a familiar song starting fast and gradually becoming slower. The children should then describe your singing as gradually becoming slower. Follow the same procedure starting slow and gradually becoming faster.

4. Have the children join you singing the song both ways (fast to slower, slow to faster). They should step to the beat (in place) as they sing to show recognition of the music gradually becoming faster and slower.

5. Play the recording of "Tempo Game." Ask the children to move their fingers (both hands) on their knees, tables, or desks in response to what they hear to show recognition of the music gradually becoming faster or slower. Model finger movement for those children who may have difficulty recognizing the changes in tempo.

6. Invite the children to join you in moving creatively to "Tempo Game." Stress the need to listen carefully and to pause in movement when the music pauses. Creeping movements might be appropriate as the music begins slow; motions might gradually become quicker and more energetic as the music becomes faster. For other playings of the music, encourage the children to move in ways different from the ways they moved during the first experience with the piece.

Materials and Equipment

- CD player

- recording of No. 16, "Tempo Game"

- drum with mallet

- selected familiar song

Related National Standards

PreK   Content Standard 1, Achievement Standard 1a
        Content Standard 3, Achievement Standard 3b, 3c
        Content Standard 4, Achievement Standard 4b

K–4   Content Standard 1, Achievement Standard 1b
        Content Standard 6, Achievement Standard 6b, 6e

Extra-Terrestrial Timbre Creatures

The children move creatively to show recognition of different musical timbres.

The Music Track 17

Extra-Terrestrial Timbre Creatures (2:01 minutes). Three bell-like signal sounds are heard. The first creature's music begins and includes fast, jerky, uneven xylophone-like sounds; the second creature's music is next and includes low-pitched, long, spooky, slow sounds; the third creature's music includes galloping, fast, short, mysterious sounds. After the three sections of music are heard, they are presented again in the same order.

Musical Understanding Focus

Guide the children to focus on the following understandings as they listen to "Extra-Terrestrial Timbre Creatures."

- Voices have unique, recognizable qualities (*timbres*).

- Instruments and sound-producing objects can be recognized by the qualities (timbres) of their sounds.

- *Sections* of music can be recognized by their sound qualities (timbres).

- Sections of music can be heard and then heard again in the same order.

- Movements can be used to show recognition of different musical timbres.

Activities

1. Have five children stand in front of your group and take turns giving their names and then saying, "I like hot dogs!" Ask those listening and watching to try to remember what each child's voice sounds like. Then, with the five children located behind a barrier—or from behind the group of listeners—randomly point to each of the five children and have them say "I like hot dogs!" without giving their names. The other children are to give the name of each child after each speaks. Play the game with a different group of five children. Guide them to understand that they recognized classmates by their voice qualities (timbres).

2. Play other timbre games using rhythm instruments and sound-producing objects. Show several different instruments and objects, name them, and let the children take turns making sounds with them. Then have a child—out of sight of the other children—play each instrument or object one-by-one. As each is played, the children listening are to name the instrument or object they heard.

3. Have the children stand and find a place for movement. Signal when they should begin moving and when they should stop. First, ask them to move with jerky, funny movements. Then ask them to move with very slow, smooth, spooky movements. Next, ask them to move with fast, short, strange movements. Then have them repeat all three kinds of movements.

4. Explain to the children that they are going to hear music for three extra-terrestrial creatures (let them describe what an extra-terrestrial creature might look like—they might even draw and color one!). Play "Extra-Terrestrial Timbre Creatures" and ask them to listen. After they hear the music, ask them to imagine that they are extra-terrestrial creatures and to move creatively to the music. Let them decide whether to use the movements they did earlier or make up new movements.

5. For another playing of "Extra-Terrestrial Timbre Creatures," ask them to move in response to what they hear. Ask them later to explain how they knew when to change the kind of movement they were using. Also ask them if, after they heard the music for the three creatures, the same music was heard again and in the same order.

Materials and Equipment

- CD player

- recording of No. 17, "Extra-Terrestrial Timbre Creatures"

- assorted rhythm instruments

- assorted sound-producing objects

Related National Standards

PreK   Content Standard 3, Achievement Standard 3b, 3c
Content Standard 4, Achievement Standard 4b

K–4   Content Standard 6, Achievement Standard 6a, 6b, 6d, 6e

---

Pitch and Tempo Flying Adventure

The children move creatively to music that becomes higher and lower and faster and slower.

The Music Track 18

Pitch and Tempo Flying Adventure (2:00 minutes). Three bell-like signal sounds are heard. Oriental-like music begins. A slow melody at a steady tempo climbs higher and higher in pitch (brief pause); the melody then climbs down lower and lower in pitch (brief pause); the melody begins slow and climbs higher and this time becomes faster (brief pause); the melody begins slow and climbs down, becoming faster as it descends; the melody is now faster and gets higher faster and comes down faster; the closing section is faster yet with swooping higher and lower sounds.

Musical Understanding Focus

Guide the children to focus on the following understandings as they listen to "Pitch and Tempo Flying Adventure."

- Voices can be used to make higher- and lower-pitched sliding sounds.

- Voices can be used to make faster and slower sliding sounds.

- Objects can be used to represent higher and lower and faster and slower sounds.

- Movements can be used to show recognition of higher- and lower-pitches, and of faster and slower sounds heard in music.

Activities

1. Invite the children to draw and color a picture of a bird. When they are finished (they may want to cut out their birds), ask them to show how to make their birds fly up high and down low. Model flying higher and lower only if needed.

2. Ask the children to use their voices to make sliding higher and lower sounds. Model this only as needed. Ask for volunteers to take turns making their birds fly up and down while using their voices to make corresponding sliding up and down sounds (as the bird flies up, the voice slides up in pitch, and so on).

3. Next, ask them to use their bird and voice sounds to fly up and down while changing speeds (going faster and slower).

4. Without their birds, have the children in small groups stand, spread their wings (arms), and fly around the room. They should fly up and down using voice sounds to correspond with their up-and-down movements.

5. Play "Pitch and Tempo Flying Adventure" and ask the children to remain seated and to fly their birds (without voice sounds) while listening to the music. They should fly their birds up and down and faster and slower to follow the "flight" of the music's changes in pitch and tempo.

6. As you play the recording again, ask the children—as a class or in small groups without their birds and without voice sounds—to move creatively about the room as they listen to the music. They should fly higher and lower and faster and slower in response to the "flight" of the music.

Materials and Equipment

- CD player

- recording of No. 18, "Pitch and Tempo Flying Adventure"

- drawing paper

- crayons or color markers

Related National Standards

PreK	Content Standard 1, Achievement Standard 1a
	Content Standard 3, Achievement Standard 3b, 3c
	Content Standard 4, Achievement Standard 4b
K–4	Content Standard 1, Achievement Standard 1a
	Content Standard 3, Achievement Standard 3d
	Content Standard 6, Achievement Standard 6b, 6e

Procession of Kings and Servants

The children play instruments and move creatively to show recognition of contrasting sections of music.

The Music  Track 19

Procession of Kings and Servants (1:33 minutes). Three tapping signal sounds are heard. The music sounds like a royal procession and has a steady tempo; the steady tempo continues as softer music with a different melody is heard; the louder procession music is heard again; the softer section is heard again; the louder procession music is heard a final time and slows down at the end.

Musical Understanding Focus

Guide the children to focus on the following understandings as they listen to "Procession of Kings and Servants."

- Music can have a steady *beat* throughout.

- Music can have loud and soft, contrasting, and alternating *sections* of music.

- Instruments can be played to the beat and to the *loudness* levels of sections of music.

- Movement can be used to show recognition of louder and softer sections of music.

Activities

1. Ask the children to move their feet up and down on the floor to make a soft sound. Then ask them to do it louder. This time ask them to make soft voice sounds while moving their feet up and down softly, and then make loud voice sounds while moving their feet up and down loudly.

2. Give each child a pair of rhythm sticks, a tone block, a woodblock, a tambourine, or a small drum. On your signal, they should play the instruments to a steady beat you give. They should continue playing until you give a stop signal. Then have them play the

instruments to the beat, alternating between loud and soft on your signals.

3. Play "Procession of Kings and Servants" and ask the children to listen and decide if there are loud *and* soft sections in the music, or *only* loud or soft sections. Lead them to discover the loud-soft-loud-soft-loud order of the music's sections.

4. Play the recording again, and have the children play their instruments to the beat of the music to correspond with its loud and soft sections. Explain why it is important to play instruments at loudness levels that will permit them to hear the music clearly when playing along with a recording.

5. Prepare for a "procession activity" of kings and servants. It is suggested that there be four groups of children as follows:

   Group 1 Kings wearing "crowns" created from paper

   Group 2 Servants wearing hats created from paper

   Group 3 Instrument group of drums, tone blocks, woodblocks

   Group 4 Instrument group of rhythm sticks, tambourines

6. As the recording is played several more times, invite the children in Groups 1 and 2 to create movements that correspond with the five sections in the music. The suggestions that follow are for the loud and soft sections each time they occur in the music.

Louder section	*Group 1* Kings march strongly to the beat "like kings"
	Group 3 Instruments play
Softer section	*Group 2* Servants march quietly to the beat
	Group 4 Instruments play

   Give the children opportunities to participate in the four different groups.

7. For a final playing of the recording, invite all children to move creatively to the beat to show that they recognize when the loud and soft sections occur in the music. If appropriate, you may want to guide them to recognize the *form* of the music (ABABA); the melodies for A and B are different, and they alternate between loud and soft.

Materials and Equipment

- CD player

- recording of No. 19, "Procession of Kings and Servants"

- rhythm sticks, tone blocks, woodblocks with mallets, tambourines, small drums with mallets

- materials to make crowns and paper hats

Related National Standards

PreK   Content Standard 1, Achievement Standard 1a
         Content Standard 3, Achievement Standard 3b, 3c
         Content Standard 4, Achievement Standard 4b

K–4   Content Standard 2, Achievement Standard 2a, 2b, 2e
         Content Standard 6, Achievement Standard 6a, 6b, 6e

Short and Crisp, Long and Smooth

The children move creatively to show recognition of short and crisp and long and smooth sounds in music.

The Music  Track 20

Short and Crisp, Long and Smooth (1:35 minutes). Three short signal sounds are heard. Short, crisp, trombone-like sounds are heard first in a kind of march-like rhythmic setting; next, long, smooth, connected sounds are heard in a kind of floating music; then the short, crisp, trombone-like sounds are heard again; the music closes with long, smooth, floating sounds.

Musical Understanding Focus

Guide the children to focus on the following understandings as they listen to "Short and Crisp, Long and Smooth."

- Voices can be used to make short crisp sounds (*staccato*).

- Voices can be used to make long, smooth sounds (*legato*).

- Music may include short, crisp sounds and long, smooth sounds.

- Movements can be used to show recognition of short and long sounds heard in music.

Activities

1. Invite the children to use their voices to make a series of short, crisp sounds speaking the word "beep." Then ask them to make very long, smooth, connected sounds while speaking the word "zoom." Signal when to begin and end the series of "beep" and "zoom" sounds.

2. Ask the children to stand and to move their bodies in ways to illustrate short and long sounds while speaking the words "beep" and "zoom."

3. Ask for volunteers to take turns speaking other words they know that can make short and long sounds while moving their bodies to represent the short and long sounds they make.

4. Divide the children into two groups. Have one group move their bodies to represent the sections of short sounds they will hear; the other group should move their bodies to represent the sections of long sounds they will hear. Play the recording of "Short and Crisp, Long and Smooth." Signal the groups when to move and when to stop moving only if necessary.

5. Invite the children, in groups of four or five, to take turns making up a dance of short and long movements as they listen to the recording of "Short and Crisp, Long and Smooth." The goal is for them to use movement to show recognition of music consisting of short, detached sounds (*staccato*) and long, smooth sounds (*legato*).

Materials and Equipment

- CD player

- recording of No. 20, "Short and Crisp, Long and Smooth"

Related National Standards

PreK   Content Standard 1, Achievement Standard 1a
             Content Standard 3, Achievement Standard 3b, 3c
             Content Standard 4, Achievement Standard 4b

K–4   Content Standard 6, Achievement Standard 6a, 6b, 6e

Chug-along Train

The children move creatively to show recognition of music that gradually becomes faster.

The Music  Track 21

Chug-along Train (1:13 minutes). Three high-pitched signal sounds are heard. The music begins with slow, low-pitched, prominent heavy sounds that gradually become faster and shorter and then stop. Then the music begins again with heavy sounds that gradually become shorter and faster than the first time.

Musical Understanding Focus

Guide the children to focus on the following understandings as they listen to "Chug-along Train."

- Voice sounds can gradually become faster (*accelerando*).

- Movements can gradually become faster.

- Voice sounds and movements can be coordinated to become faster together.

- Movements can be used to illustrate music that gradually becomes faster.

Activities

1. Ask for volunteers to take turns walking very slowly and then gradually, bit by bit, walk faster and faster. Model this pattern of walking only if needed.

2. Find out if any of the children have watched a train pulled by a steam engine begin slowly and gradually become faster and faster. They could illustrate this by following your gestures and speaking the word "chug" over and over, gradually becoming faster.

3. Give each child—or groups of children taking turns—a pair of rhythm sticks, and have them follow your gestures to begin making tapping sounds slowly and gradually become faster and faster.

4. Invite the children to be a "train" by forming a line and placing their hands on the shoulders of the child in front of them. You could be the steam engine to lead and control the speed of the train. As the train moves, they should step slowly, saying "chug" each time they take a step, and then gradually become faster. You should signal when the train stops and starts again.

5. Have the children in groups of five or six take turns forming short trains. As they listen to "Chug-along Train," they should begin moving slowly and become faster (*accelerando*) as the music becomes faster. Remind them that the music stops and starts over again.

6. Invite the children to individually create their own "Chug-along Train" dance as they listen to the music again. Encourage them to listen closely to the music and to move to represent the train gradually becoming faster.

Materials and Equipment

- CD player

- recording of No. 21, "Chug-along Train"

- pairs of rhythm sticks

Related National Standards

PreK   Content Standard 3, Achievement Standard 3b, 3c
             Content Standard 4, Achievement Standard 4b

K–4   Content Standard 2, Achievement Standard 2a
             Content Standard 6, Achievement Standard 6b, 6e

Fast Piano, Slow Piano

**The children move creatively to show recognition of
music that gradually becomes slower.**

The Music

Fast Piano, Slow Piano (1:30 minutes). Three short, piano-like signal sounds are heard; the music begins with fast sounds that gradually slow down and stop; next, the piano-like sounds begin again playing fast and gradually slow down and stop; then the fast to slow pattern is played a third time.

Musical Understanding Focus

Guide the children to focus on the following understandings as they listen to "Fast Piano, Slow Piano."

- Objects that move can go fast and gradually slow down (*ritardando*).

- Movements of the body can be fast and then gradually slow down.

- Sounds can be played fast and gradually slower.

- Movements can be used to show recognition of music that is fast and gradually slows down.

Activities

1. Arrange to have available a toy car or another kind of push toy with wheels. In an open space, have a child give the toy a strong push and ask the children to watch. Then ask them to describe what happened. Have the toy rolled again as necessary to help the children recognize that the toy first moved fast and then slowed to a stop. Ask for several volunteers to move as the toy moved—fast, gradually slow down, and stop.

2. Have the children follow your cues and use their hands to pat their thighs very fast, then gradually slow down, and come to a stop. Guide the children to recognize that objects, movements of the body, and sounds can all begin fast and gradually slow down and stop. Then have groups of four or five children follow your cues and take turns moving in response to the thigh-patting pattern of sounds. All children should eventually participate as "mover" and "patter."

3. Give each child a pair of rhythm sticks and ask the children to follow your cues to make rhythm-stick tapping sounds that copy the sound pattern of the thigh-patting sounds.

4. Play "Fast Piano, Slow Piano." Ask the children to remain seated and to shake their hands in front of their bodies in response to what they hear. Each of the three patterns played by piano-like sounds begins fast and gradually slows down and comes to a stop.

5. As the children listen to "Fast Piano, Slow Piano" again, invite them to create their own dance of moving fast, slowing down, and coming to a stop in response to what they hear. A goal is to help them recognize that music sometimes (a) has a steady *tempo*, (b) slows down (*ritardando*), and (c) speeds up (*accelerando*).

Materials and Equipment

- CD player

- recording of No. 22, "Fast Piano, Slow Piano"

- pairs of rhythm sticks

- toy car or other push toy with wheels

Related National Standards

PreK   Content Standard 1, Achievement Standard 1c
            Content Standard 3, Achievement Standard 3b, 3c
            Content Standard 4, Achievement Standard 4b

K–4   Content Standard 2, Achievement Standard 2a, 2c
            Content Standard 6, Achievement Standard 6a, 6b, 6e

Rhythm Robots

The children move creatively to show recognition of music that has contrasting rhythm patterns.

The Music  Track 23

Rhythm Robots (2:28 minutes). Three cymbal-like tapping sounds signal that the music is about to begin; the first rhythm pattern, played mostly by drum-like sounds, begins and continues until there is a pause; a cymbal crash then introduces the second rhythm pattern, which continues until two cymbal-like tapping sounds signal a return to the first rhythm pattern; then a cymbal-like crash signals the final section, which is a return of the second rhythm pattern.

Musical Understanding Focus

Guide the children to focus on the following understandings as they listen to "Rhythm Robots."

- *Rhythm patterns* can be heard, recalled, and played back.

- The rhythm of a melody of a song can be clapped (*melodic rhythm*).

- Movements can be used to imitate imaginary movements of a robot.

- Movements can be used to reveal recognition of contrasting rhythm patterns heard in music.

Activities

1. Invite the children to take turns patting their thighs or tapping a tabletop or desk and make up a rhythm of some kind. Model patting or tapping a rhythm only if needed. Simple patterns like *tap* silence *tap tap tap tap* silence *tap tap tap* could be used in the initial stages.

2. Play a rhythm echo game where you and the children take turns tapping a short pattern. After tapping a pattern, signal the children to begin and try together or individually to tap the pattern they just heard.

3. Have the children sing a familiar song they like, and ask them to clap each time they sing a word or syllable. They clap on each sound they sing, or in other words, clap the rhythm of the song's melody. Later, signal when they are to begin and have them clap the rhythm of the song's melody *without* singing aloud. They should sing *inside themselves* while clapping its rhythm.

4. Ask for volunteers to take turns showing how a robot might move.

5. Play "Rhythm Robots" and ask the children to remain seated but to move their arms and hands like robots to the rhythms they hear in the music.

6. Divide the children into two groups. Group 1 should be on one side of the room, Group 2 on the other side. As they hear "Rhythm Robots" again, Group 1 should move like robots to the first pattern, Group 2 like robots to the second pattern. Group 2 remains still during the Group 1 pattern; Group 1 remains still during the Group 2 pattern. The order of movements is Group 1, Group 2, Group 1, Group 2. The goal is to have them recognize when their pattern occurs and to show their recognition through movement without your help.

7. Play "Rhythm Robots" again and invite the children to make up their own dance to all sections of the music.

Materials and Equipment

- CD player

- recording of No. 23, "Rhythm Robots"

Related National Standards

PreK   Content Standard 1, Achievement Standard 1b, 1c
            Content Standard 3, Achievement Standard 3b, 3c
            Content Standard 4, Achievement Standard 4b

K–4   Content Standard 1, Achievement Standard 1c
            Content Standard 6, Achievement Standard 6a, 6b, 6e

Swooping Sound Contours

The children move creatively to show recognition of upward and downward pitch contours.

The Music  Track 24

Swooping Sound Contours (1:30 minutes). Two bell-like sounds signal that the music is about to begin; the music begins with fast, running-like sounds; the sounds gradually become higher and higher and then begin to swoop up and down, suggesting the flight of a bird; more sounds gradually join in for more swooping sounds; the music then slows down and stops.

Musical Understanding Focus

Guide the children to focus on the following understandings as they listen to "Swooping Sound Contours."

- The voice can be used to make sounds that slide up and down in pitch.

- Arm movements can be used to match the up-and-down pitch movement of voice sounds.

- Arm movements can be used to trace the up-and-down pitch movement of melodies of songs.

- Voice sounds can be used to approximate the shape of graphic notation.

- Movement can be used to show recognition of the upward and downward pitch movement of music.

Activities

1. Use your voice on a syllable sound such as *lee* or *la* and make sounds that slide up and down from higher to lower to higher, etc. Then invite the children to join you in making

sliding voice sounds.

2. With one arm extended in front of you, use your voice to slide up and down, but this time move your arm up and down to correspond with the up-and-down movement of your voice. Gradually help the children to move their arms to the up-and-down movements of their voices.

3. Draw simple contours like the one that follows on a chalkboard or on a large sheet of drawing paper. As you trace beneath each contour with your finger or a pointer, ask the children to make sliding voice sounds to *read* the drawings.

4. Have the children sing one of their favorite and most familiar songs. As they sing, they should move their arms up and down to follow the up-and-down pitch movement of the song's melody.

5. Play "Swooping Sound Contours" and ask the children to remain seated and try to move their arms to follow the upward and downward pitch motion of the music. For another playing of the music, ask the children to stand and to use reaching-up-high and bending-down-low movements to try to follow the up-and-down motion of the music (*contour*).

6. As the children listen to "Swooping Sound Contours" again, invite them to individually make up their own dance to follow the upward and downward motion of the music. The goal is to help them learn to recognize—and reveal their recognition—of the music's upward and downward pitch motion.

Materials and Equipment

- CD player

- recording of No. 24, "Swooping Sound Contours"

- chalkboard or large sheet of drawing paper

Related National Standards

PreK   Content Standard 1, Achievement Standard 1a
             Content Standard 3, Achievement Standard 3b, 3c
             Content Standard 4, Achievement Standard 4b

K–4   Content Standard 3, Achievement Standard 3d
             Content Standard 6, Achievement Standard 6b, 6e

Big, Hungry Dinosaur

The children move creatively to represent characteristics of music they hear.

The Music Track 25

Big, Hungry Dinosaur (1:04 minutes). Three strange sounds signal the music is about to begin; slow, mysterious, spooky, low-pitched sounds representing the slow movements of a big dinosaur are heard; the music portrays a dinosaur taking a very slow walk to look for food; twice the music pauses to suggest the dinosaur stops to look around; after each pause, the music continues and the dinosaur's walk finally ends.

Musical Understanding Focus

Guide the children to focus on the following understandings as they listen to "Big, Hungry Dinosaur."

- Musical sounds can be very low-pitched, slow, mysterious, or spooky.

- Movements can illustrate the slow, searching walk of a dinosaur.

- Movements can reveal recognition of slow, low-pitched, long, stopping and starting sounds.

Activities

It is suggested that "Big, Hungry Dinosaur" and No. 26, "Tiny, Dancing Mouse," be used both separately and together so the children can identify ways the two selections contrast with each other.

1. Invite the children to tell about a dinosaur they have seen on television, in a storybook, or in a museum. Then ask several volunteers to take turns moving like a big dinosaur.

2. Encourage the children to share their ideas about what they think music for a big, hungry dinosaur might sound like. Will the music be fast? Will it be slow? Will it have mostly high or low sounds (*pitch*)? Will it be spooky? Will it have a lot of short, quick sounds (*staccato*), or a lot of long, smooth sounds (*legato*)? Following the sharing of ideas, invite other volunteers to take turns moving like a dinosaur.

3. Play "Big, Hungry Dinosaur." Afterward, ask the children to describe what they heard.

4. Ask for several volunteers to move to the music as you play "Big, Hungry Dinosaur" again. Especially suggest that they stop moving to look around for food each time there is a pause in the music.

5. Play the recording again and invite all the children to create their own dinosaur walk dance.

Materials and Equipment

- CD player

- recording of No. 25, "Big, Hungry Dinosaur"

Related National Standards

PreK   Content Standard 3, Achievement Standard 3b, 3c
Content Standard 4, Achievement Standard 4b

K–4   Content Standard 6, Achievement Standard 6b, 6c, 6e

Tiny, Dancing Mouse

The children move creatively to represent characteristics of music they hear.

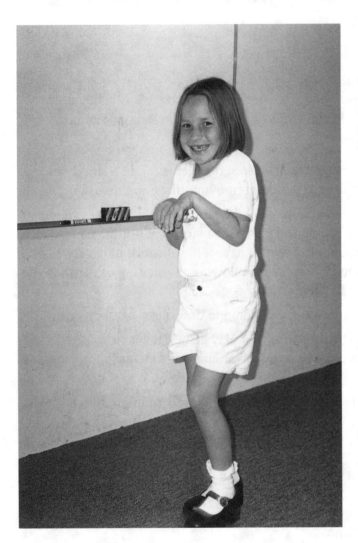

The Music  Track 26

Tiny, Dancing Mouse (1:02 minutes). Three soft, bell-like sounds signal that the music is about to begin; the music begins and consists of sounds that suggest a quick, playful, light, stopping and starting, jerky dance; these sounds are later joined by squeaking mouse sounds; the music ends just as it began—quick, light, and playful.

Musical Understanding Focus

Guide the children to focus on the following understandings as they listen to "Tiny, Dancing Mouse."

- Voices can make high-pitched, short (*staccato*), squeaking sounds.

- Music may include high-pitched, short, squeaking sounds.

- Movement can be used to portray the playful dance of a tiny mouse.

- Movement can be used to show recognition of quick, short, jerky music.

Activities

It is suggested that "Tiny, Dancing Mouse" and "Big, Hungry Dinosaur" be used both separately and together so the children can identify ways the two selections contrast with each other.

1. Ask the children if they have ever heard the squeaking sound of a mouse. Then invite them to use their voices to make short, high-pitched, squeaking sounds. When they catch on to the idea, signal when they should begin to produce a "symphony" of mouse squeaking sounds and when they should stop.

2. Have half of the children make squeaking sounds as the other half individually portrays, through movement, mice doing a playful dance. Signal when the "squeaks" and "mice" are to begin and end the dance.

3. Encourage the children to share their ideas about what they think music for a tiny, dancing mouse would sound like. Will the music be fast or slow? Will it have mostly high or mostly low sounds? Will it sound spooky, playful, sad? Will it have a lot of short, quick sounds (*staccato*) or a lot of long, slow sounds? After they share their ideas, play "Tiny, Dancing Mouse"; ask them later to decide if the music fits the dance of a little mouse and explain why they think so.

4. Play "Tiny, Dancing Mouse" again and ask the children to make squeaking sounds to accompany the music. If possible, make a recording of the music with their accompanying squeaking sounds. Play back the recording and ask them to describe why they do or do not like the sound of the music that includes their squeaks. Ask the question even if no recording was made.

5. Play "Tiny, Dancing Mouse" again and ask the children to individually create their own dance for the music. Squeaking sounds while dancing may be appropriate.

Materials and Equipment

- CD player

- recording of No. 26, "Tiny, Dancing Mouse"

- audiocassette player, microphone, and blank tape (optional)

Related National Standards

PreK   Content Standard 1, Achievement Standard 1a
Content Standard 2, Achievement Standard 2c
Content Standard 3, Achievement Standard 3b, 3c
Content Standard 4, Achievement Standard 4b

K–4   Content Standard 3, Achievement Standard 3d
Content Standard 6, Achievement Standard 6b, 6c, 6e

Melody Again and Again

The children move creatively to show recognition of a melody played by different instruments.

The Music  Track 27

Melody Again and Again (1:42 minutes). Three piano-like sounds signal that the music is about to begin; a melody is played first by piano-like sounds; the same melody is played next by trumpet-like sounds; the same melody is then played by clarinet-like sounds; string-like sounds play the same melody for a final time.

Musical Understanding Focus

Guide the children to focus on the following understandings as they listen to "Melody Again and Again."

- Different kinds of musical instruments look different and sound different.

- Each musical instrument has a unique tone quality (*timbre*) that distinguishes it from other instruments.

- The same melody can be played by different kinds of musical instruments.

- Movement can be used to show recognition of changes in timbre.

Activities

1. Ask the children to name as many musical instruments as they can. List these on the chalkboard or on chart paper. If you have picture books or poster pictures of instruments, have them available for the children to see.

2. Explain that the different kinds of musical instruments not only look different but also sound different. Have several children briefly play instruments you have in your classroom, such as resonator bells, drum, jingle bells, and rhythm sticks. Point out that we can learn to recognize these instruments without looking at them because of the way they sound (tone quality, or timbre).

3. Play "Melody Again and Again." Afterward, ask the children to tell about anything in the music they noticed. Lead them to recognize that the same melody was presented four times but was played each time by different kinds of sounds (piano-, trumpet-, clarinet-, and string-like sounds).

4. Play "Melody Again and Again" again. This time show the pictures of the instruments or name the instrument as each begins playing. For another playing of the recording, suggest that the children move to the music in different ways as the four different kinds of sounds are heard. For instance, they could stand in place and

Piano   swing or sway from side to side to the beat

Trumpet   march quietly to the beat

Clarinet   bend up and down to the beat

Strings   swing arms to the beat

5. For another playing of "Melody Again and Again," invite the children to individually create their own "timbre dance" in response to what they hear. You might suggest that they consider moving a different way each time the melody is played by a different kind of instrument.

Materials and Equipment

- CD player

- recording of No. 27, "Melody Again and Again"

- resonator bells, drum, jingle bells, rhythm sticks, and other instruments

- pictures of musical instruments

- chalkboard or chart paper

Related National Standards

PreK   Content Standard 1, Achievement Standard 1c
                Content Standard 3, Achievement Standard 3b, 3c
                Content Standard 4, Achievement Standard 4b

K–4   Content Standard 6, Achievement Standard 6d, 6e

Flyers and Marchers

The children move creatively to show recognition of contrasting sections of music in ABABA form.

The Music  Track 28

Flyers and Marchers (1:29 minutes). Three tapping sounds signal the music is about to begin; a flowing, pleasant, legato-style melody is played by clarinet-like sounds; next, marching sounds featuring the snare drum and cymbals are heard; the flowing clarinet melody returns; the snare drum and cymbals return; the melody played by clarinet is heard a final time.

Musical Understanding Focus

Guide the children to focus on the following understandings as they listen to "Flyers and Marchers."

- Music may include sections that *contrast* with each other.

- The order in which different *sections* of music are presented can be described as its *form*.

- Movement can be used to show recognition of contrasting sections of music.

- Movement can be used to illustrate music that has an ABABA form.

Activities

1. Ask the children to take turns in small groups and show how they can march. Ask those watching to describe the different kinds of marching they see.

2. Next, ask the children to take turns in small groups running slowly and quietly while "flapping" to show how a beautiful bird might fly.

3. Divide the children into two groups—one group to march, the other group to fly like a beautiful bird. Explain how you will signal the "marchers" and "flyers" when to begin and when to stop doing their movement. When they are able to follow your signals, have them move in their two groups again using this pattern: flyers-marchers-flyers-marchers-flyers. Ask them afterward to give the order in which the two kinds of movements occurred. Which group moved first? Which group moved second? etc.

4. Play "Flyers and Marchers." After they hear the music, ask the children if they could tell when the music suggested flying movements and marching movements. (If pictures of clarinet, snare drum, and cymbals are available, display the pictures and play the music again. As the children listen, they should point to the picture of each instrument when it is featured in the music.)

5. Invite the children in two groups to move to the music. The order is flyers (clarinet), marchers (snare drum, cymbals), flyers (clarinet), marchers (snare drum, cymbals), flyers (clarinet).

6. Point out, or lead the children to discover (as appropriate), the order of the events in the music that constitute the music's ABABA form (flyers-marchers-flyers-marchers-flyers).

Materials and Equipment

- CD player

- recording of No. 28, "Flyers and Marchers"

- pictures of clarinet, snare drum, cymbals

Related National Standards

PreK   Content Standard 3, Achievement Standard 3b, 3c
                Content Standard 4, Achievement Standard 4b

K–4   Content Standard 6, Achievement Standard 6b, 6d, 6e

Melodies Alone, Then Together

The children move creatively to show recognition of two melodies heard alone and then together.

The Music  Track 29

Melodies Alone, Then Together (1:38 minutes). Three short sounds signal the music is about to begin; first, a slow, smooth melody is heard; next, a contrasting slow, smooth melody is heard; the first melody returns; the second melody returns; the first and second melodies are then heard together.

Musical Understanding Focus

Guide the children to focus on the following understandings as they listen to "Melodies Alone, Then Together."

- Music may include contrasting melodies.

- Melodies may be slow and smooth.

- Melodies may be heard separately and sometimes together in music.

- Movement can be used to show recognition of slow, smooth melodies.

Activities

1. Play "Melodies Alone, Then Together" and ask a small group of children to try using running, hopping, and jumping movements to find out if any of the three movements seems to fit the music. Encourage those who are watching to decide if any of the movements seems to fit.

2. Play "Melodies Alone, Then Together" again and have a different small group of children try using jerky, shaking, and marching movements to find out if any of these three seems to fit the music. Watchers should continue looking for a movement that seems to fit.

3. For a third playing of "Melodies Alone, Then Together," have another small group of children try bending and swinging or swaying to the beat to find out if these movements will fit the music. Afterward, invite the children to name from the nine different movements used those that seem to fit the music, and tell why they think so. Lead them to recognize that slow, smooth melodies suggest slow, smooth movements.

4. Divide the children into two groups—one group on one side of the room, the other group on the other side. Use the information that describes the music to signal the two groups when to move. Group 1 will move to the first melody, Group 2 to the second melody. The order of movements by the groups will be

Group 1—Group 2—Group 1—Group 2—Groups 1 and 2 together

You may later want to play the recording again and let them listen to the music to decide when their group should move.

5. For a final playing of "Melodies Alone, Then Together," invite the children to create their own dance and to use movements of their choice to represent the melodies in the music.

Materials and Equipment

- CD player

- recording of No. 29, "Melodies Alone, Then Together"

Related National Standards

PreK Content Standard 3, Achievement Standard 3b, 3c
Content Standard 4, Achievement Standard 4b

K–4 Content Standard 6, Achievement Standard 6a, 6b, 6e

Music for Body Sound Accompaniment

The children use body sounds to create an accompaniment to music.

The Music  Track 30

Music for Body Sound Accompaniment (1:08 minutes). Three quick, short sounds signal the music will begin; the music is march-like, has a steady beat throughout, and has no melodies; it provides a musical setting for adding rhythm sounds as an accompaniment.

Musical Understanding Focus

Guide the children to focus on the following understandings as they listen to "Music for Body Sound Accompaniment."

- A variety of body sounds can be made by stepping, clapping, and tapping and patting different parts of the body (*timbre*).

- A variety of body sounds can be performed to a steady *beat*.

- A variety of body sounds can be performed in time with the beat of music.

- Body sounds can be used to create a background of sound (*accompaniment*) for recorded music.

Activities

1. Ask the children to stand and to march "in place" to the beat you give. You could start the marching by saying "1, 2; 1, 2; ready go," and have them count aloud 1, 2; 1, 2 as they march.

2. As you signal the children to begin marching in place again, ask them to clap their hands together on each 1, 2; 1, 2. The sounds of the hand claps should be made to match the sounds of their stepping feet.

3. Without having them count aloud, ask them to march in place again. This time divide the children into three groups. One group should make clapping sounds to match their feet sounds, a second group should pat their tummies to match their feet sounds, the third group should bend slightly and pat their thighs to match their feet sounds.

4. Play "Music for Body Sound Accompaniment" and invite the children to march in place and to explore and use a variety of body sounds of their choice (hand claps, thigh pats, tummy pats, finger snaps, accented feet steps, "bottom" pats, etc.) to match the beats of the music or to make up rhythms that will fit the music. Explain that an accompaniment in music serves as a background, and background sounds should be softer than the music they are listening to (foreground).

5. As you play "Music for Body Sound Accompaniment" three more times, have the children in three groups take turns making up their own dance consisting of marching movements (marching about the room, not in place) and performing body sounds that will accompany and "fit" the music. As the other children watch, they should notice unique ways those who are dancing are making body sounds and the kinds of movements they are using.

Materials and Equipment

- CD player

- recording of No. 30, "Music for Body Sound Accompaniment"

Related National Standards

PreK   Content Standard 3, Achievement Standard 3b, 3c
             Content Standard 4, Achievement Standard 4b

K–4   Content Standard 3, Achievement Standard 3a
             Content Standard 6, Achievement Standard 6b, 6e

Music That Goes Home

The children move creatively to show recognition of music that returns to a home tone (tonic pitch).

The Music  Track 31

Music That Goes Home (1:11 minutes). Two sounds signal that the music will begin; this beautiful music was composed to create in the listener a deliberate and unmistakable feeling for a return to the *tonic pitch* (or *home tone*) at the very end; the music slows near the end and then dramatically comes to rest on its home tone.

Musical Understanding Focus

Guide the children to focus on the following understandings as they listen to "Music That Goes Home."

- Music can sometimes feel complete or incomplete.

- Music that comes to rest on its tonic pitch, or home tone, feels complete.

- Some body movements may not fit the expressive style of music.

- Movement can be used to illustrate the expressive nature of music.

Activities

1. Select the following bells from a resonator bell set and line them up as shown.

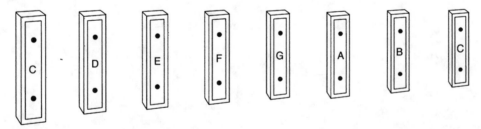

Use a mallet and produce one sound on each bell, starting on the lower C and proceeding up to the higher C, then back down to the lower C. Play the same thing again, but when coming down this time, stop on the D. Ask the children if it sounds complete or incomplete without the last C. They will naturally want to hear the last sound. You could let them take turns playing the bells up and down and have them decide whether or not to play the last bell (C).

2. Sing "Twinkle, Twinkle, Little Star" for the children and withhold singing the last word (note) at the end of the song. Afterward, ask them if the song sounded complete or incomplete. Then lead them in singing the song. As they approach the end of the song, signal them to stop singing and to pause on the next to the last word (note); then on your next signal, they should sing the final word (tonic pitch or home tone). You might try this on other songs such as "This Old Man" and "Three Blind Mice."

3. Play "Music That Goes Home" and ask the children to listen and to be ready later to describe what they hear. You could use prompter questions such as, Was the music beautiful? Did the music sound complete? Was the music fast with a lot of short sounds, or smooth with a lot of long sounds? How did the music make you feel?

4. Have a small group of children move to the music as you play "Music That Goes Home" again. Afterward, ask the children who were watching to name the different kinds of movements they observed. Prompter questions (such as, Did anybody use shaking movements? What kinds of movements did you see? Why do you think some movements fit the music but others do not?) may help the children recall what they saw.

5. Invite all the children to independently create their own dance for another playing of "Music That Goes Home." Especially ask them to strike a pose with their arms outstretched when they hear the final sound (tonic pitch or home tone) at the end.

Materials and Equipment

- CD player

- recording of No. 31, "Music That Goes Home"

- resonator bell set

Related National Standards

PreK Content Standard 3, Achievement Standard 3b, 3c
        Content Standard 4, Achievement Standard 4a, 4b

K–4   Content Standard 6, Achievement Standard 6b, 6c, 6e

One Sound, More Than One Sound

The children move creatively to show recognition of when one kind of sound and more than one kind of sound occur in music.

The Music  Track 32

One Sound, More Than One Sound (1:13 minutes). Three sounds signal the music will begin; a melody played by piano-like sounds alone (no accompaniment) is heard first; then the same melody is played by piano with an accompaniment; next, the same melody played by piano alone (no accompaniment) returns; finally, the same melody is played again by piano but with an accompaniment.

Musical Understanding Focus

Guide the children to focus on the following understandings as they listen to "One Sound, More Than One Sound."

- Music may include only one kind of sound.

- Music may include more than one kind of sound.

- Music may include *sections* that have one kind of sound and sections that have more than one kind of sound (*simultaneous tones*).

- Movement can be used to show recognition of sections in music that include one kind of sound and sections that include more than one kind of sound (simultaneous tones).

Activities

1. Select a poem and read it aloud to the children. Then read it again. This time, as you read it aloud, tap the beat of the poem with your foot on the floor and with your fingertips on a book. Then ask the children to tell you how the sound of the reading the first time (only voice sound) and the sound of the reading the second time (voice, foot tap, finger tap sounds) was different.

2. Sing a simple song (such as "Michael, Row the Boat Ashore") that has more than one verse. If it has two verses, sing one verse alone, then sing the other verse while shaking a jingle clog to the beat or tapping a tone block to the beat. If it has more than two verses, alternate singing alone and singing while playing an instrument for the different verses. Then ask the children to tell how the performance of the song was like or different from

the performance of the poem (sometimes one kind of sound at a time, sometimes more than one kind of sound at a time).

3. Play "One Sound, More Than One Sound" and ask the children to listen and to be ready later to describe what they heard. Prompter questions could be asked such as, What did you hear in the music? Did you hear only one kind of sound in the music? Did you hear more than one kind of sound in the music?

4. Divide the children into two groups. As they listen to "One Sound, More Than One Sound" again, Group 1 should move only when there is only one kind of sound heard in the music; Group 2 should move only when there is more than one kind of sound heard in the music. The groups should use movements they believe fit the music. Afterward, have them tell you the order the musical events were heard.

   Group 1 (one kind of sound, piano alone)

   Group 2 (more than one kind of sound, piano with accompaniment)

   Group 1 (one kind of sound, piano alone)

   Group 2 (more than one kind of sound, piano with accompaniment)

   The goal of this activity is to help the children develop their listening skills to recognize when one kind of sound is heard and when more than one kind of sound is heard in music.

5. For another playing, invite the children to create their own dance to the music. Encourage them to use movements that seem to fit the music but to use different movements for sections when one kind of sound is heard and when more than one kind of sound is heard.

Materials and Equipment

- CD player

- recording of No. 32, "One Sound, More Than One Sound"

- selected poem

- selected song

- jingle clog or tone block

Related National Standards

PreK   Content Standard 1, Achievement Standard 1a
        Content Standard 3, Achievement Standard 3b, 3c
        Content Standard 4, Achievement Standard 4b

K–4   Content Standard 6, Achievement Standard 6a, 6b, 6e

Laughing Sound Contours

The children laugh and move creatively to the rhythms and pitch contours of laughing sounds.

The Music  Track 33

Laughing Sound Contours (1:31 minutes). Four signal sounds are heard; then, two ducks sitting by a mud pond begin to laugh; horses hear the ducks laughing and decide to join in the fun; gradually, other animals begin to laugh along with the ducks and horses and join in to create a "symphony" of laughing sounds.

Musical Understanding Focus

Guide the children to focus on the following understandings as they listen to "Laughing Sound Contours."

- Laughing sounds may have different kinds of qualities (*timbres*).

- Laughing sounds may have different *rhythms*.

- Laughing sounds may have different *tempos* (speed).

- Laughing sounds usually have descending pitch *contours*.

Activities

1. Invite the children one-by-one to demonstrate ways they can laugh.

2. After they hear four or five kinds of laughs, ask them to explain how the laughs sound different or alike (faster and slower, higher or lower in pitch, longer or shorter sounds, louder or softer sounds, etc.). Do this several times with other children making laughing sounds.

3. Ask for volunteers to take turns making different kinds of laughing sounds (fast, slow, loud, soft, long, short, scary, silly, funny, robotic, etc.).

4. Invite volunteers to take turns laughing in a way they choose and to move either parts of their bodies or their entire bodies in some way they believe matches the way they are laughing.

5. Play the recording "Laughing Sound Contours" and ask the children to remain silent and to move their bodies to the laughing sounds as they listen.

6. Play the recording again and ask them to join in with the recording by creating laughing sounds they think other animals might make. They should all move their bodies in some way to match the kinds of laughing sounds they make.

Materials and Equipment

- CD player

- recording of No. 33, "Laughing Sound Contours"

Related National Standards

PreK Content Standard 1, Achievement Standard 1a
Content Standard 2, Achievement Standard 2a
Content Standard 3, Achievement Standard 3b, 3c
Content Standard 4, Achievement Standard 4b

K–4 Content Standard 3, Achievement Standard 3d
Content Standard 6, Achievement Standard 6b, 6e

Here Comes the Parade

The children move creatively to show recognition of *crescendo* and *decrescendo*.

The Music  Track 34

Here Comes the Parade (1:50 minutes). Two signal sounds are heard; percussion-like instruments begin playing softly; the band joins the percussion instruments and the music gradually becomes louder as the band approaches; the band passes by; and the music gradually becomes softer as the band marches away.

Musical Understanding Focus

Guide the children to focus on the following understandings as they listen to "Here Comes the Parade."

- Music that gradually becomes louder is an example of *crescendo* (⬅).
- Music that gradually becomes softer is an example of *decrescendo* (➡).
- Movement can be used to show recognition of *crescendo* and *decrescendo*.

Activities

1. Invite the children to take turns describing parades they have seen. Encourage them to name the kinds of things they saw (marchers, horseback riders, bands, etc.).

2. Ask them if while waiting for the parade to arrive they could hear a band playing in the distance, and whether the band gradually became louder as it got closer.

3. You might illustrate this by having three children play instruments (drum, rhythm sticks, woodblock) to a beat, starting outside the classroom, marching into and around the classroom, then returning to the outside area. Help the children recognize that the sounds gradually became louder as they entered the classroom, softer as they left.

4. Play "Here Comes the Parade" and ask the children to listen and later describe what they heard. Help them recognize the pattern of *crescendo* and *decrescendo*.

5. Play the recording again and invite the children to create their own marching dance to illustrate *crescendo* and *decrescendo*. Their marching (stepping) sounds could begin soft, gradually become louder, then gradually softer. Body movements (stepping higher, arm movements) could also be used to illustrate the *loudness* pattern of the music.

Materials and Equipment

- CD player

- recording of No. 34, "Here Comes the Parade"

- drum with mallet, rhythm sticks, woodblock with mallet

Related National Standards

PreK Content Standard 1, Achievement Standard 1d
Content Standard 2, Achievement Standard 2b
Content Standard 3, Achievement Standard 3b, 3c
Content Standard 4, Achievement Standard 4b

K–4 Content Standard 2, Achievement Standard 2b, 2e, 2f
Content Standard 6, Achievement Standard 6a, 6b, 6c, 6e

Cool, Jazzy Walk

**The children move creatively in response to
the style and beat of the music.**

The Music

Track 35

Cool, Jazzy Walk (2:03 minutes). The music begins with percussion-like instruments playing rhythms that suggest a casual, walking beat; a flute-like instrument adds a melody to the rhythms, then a clarinet-like sound joins in with the instruments already playing; piano-like sounds are then added to the "combo" as all instruments play jazzy parts together to a steady beat; the music continues and gradually fades away.

Musical Understanding Focus

Guide the children to focus on the following understandings as they listen to "Cool, Jazzy Walk."

- Walking and stepping can be done in time with the steady *beat* of music.

- There are many different ways to walk in time with the steady beat of music.

- Walking movements can be used to show recognition of the expressive nature of music.

Activities

1. Ask for volunteers to take turns showing different ways they can walk. Should prompters be needed, you might suggest such things as walking forward, backward, sideward, bouncy, heavy, tippi-toe, on heels of feet, cool, angry, and others.

2. Clap your hands or tap a drum to a steady, not-too-fast walking beat. Invite the children as a group, or taking turns in small groups, to walk different ways to the beat you play. Encourage them to step with their feet touching the floor in time with your claps or taps.

3. For more claps or drum taps, ask for volunteers to do a jazzy walk to the beats you play. (Whatever they consider to be "jazzy" should be accepted.)

4. Play "Cool, Jazzy Walk" and ask the children to softly pat one hand on their thigh to the beat of the music. Encourage them to listen carefully and to make their patting sounds in time with the beat they hear.

5. As you play "Cool, Jazzy Walk" a few more times, give groups of two or three volunteers opportunities to create a cool, jazzy walk to perform with the music. You could have each group begin with the percussion sounds at the beginning of the music or point to individual children to begin as the different instruments are added to the combo.

6. You might use the music to have a "jazzy walk contest" and let the children vote for whom they believe did the jazziest walk.

Materials and Equipment

- CD player

- recording of No. 35, "Cool, Jazzy Walk"

- drum with mallet (optional)

Related National Standards

PreK   Content Standard 3, Achievement Standard 3b, 3c
                   Content Standard 4, Achievement Standard 4b

K–4   Content Standard 6, Achievement Standard 6c, 6e

Melodies with and without Accompaniment

The children listen and move creatively to show recognition of melodies with and without an accompaniment.

The Music  Track 36

Melodies with and without Accompaniment (1:59 minutes). The music begins with clarinet-like sounds playing a nice melody alone, without an accompaniment. After the melody is heard two times, piano-like sounds are heard playing a different melody, but with the clarinet playing an accompaniment part in the background. Next, a third kind of sound (sustained chords) adds more accompaniment. Finally, the clarinet again plays the original melody alone two times without accompaniment.

Musical Understanding Focus

Guide the children to focus on the following understandings as they listen to "Melodies with and without Accompaniment."

- A melody heard may return again after different melodies are heard (*recurrence*).

- A melody played or sung alone can be called a *solo*.

- A melody sung by a group of singers who sing the same thing at the same time is *unison* singing.

- Melodies can be performed with and without an *accompaniment*.

Activities

1. Invite a volunteer to sing alone one verse of "Old MacDonald" or another familiar song.

2. Ask all the children in the group to sing together the verse of the selected song.

3. Have half of the group tap a book or tabletop to a steady beat while the other half sings the verse of the selected song. Afterward, help them to recognize how their three performances were different.

- a volunteer singing the song alone (solo, without accompaniment)

- all singing the song together at the same time (unison singing, without accompaniment)

- half of the group singing the song and half of the group tapping a steady beat (unison, with accompaniment)

4. Play "Melodies with and without Accompaniment" and ask the children to listen to find out if what they hear is in any way like their three performances of the selected song. Guide them to recognize

- the clarinet played a melody alone (solo, without accompaniment)

- the piano played different melodies (solo, with clarinet accompaniment)

- the clarinet played a melody alone (solo, without accompaniment)

5. Invite small groups to take turns creating a dance to move to the music as you play the recording again. One group should move only when the clarinet plays alone; the other group moves when more than one kind of instrument is playing. Cue a group when to begin only if needed. Guide them to recognize that the melody they heard first returns for the ending section of the music.

6. For another playing of the recording, invite all the children to move in a way they choose to create their own dance for the music.

Materials and Equipment

- CD player

- recording of No. 36, "Melodies with and without Accompaniment"

Related National Standards

PreK Content Standard 1, Achievement Standard 1a, 1b
Content Standard 3, Achievement Standard 3b, 3c
Content Standard 4, Achievement Standard 4b

K–4 Content Standard 1, Achievement Standard 1b, 1e
Content Standard 6, Achievement Standard 6a, 6b, 6c, 6e

Busy Bee

The children move creatively to show recognition of higher and lower pitch contours.

The Music  Track 37

Busy Bee (1:15 minutes). Three signal sounds are heard; the bee then begins its flight in search of sweet nectar; it flies up and down and hovers at times while extracting nectar from plants; the up-and-down flight continues with more hovering sounds.

Musical Understanding Focus

Guide the children to focus on the following understandings as they listen to "Busy Bee."

- Voices can be used to make sliding sounds of higher and lower *pitch*.

- An arm can be used to trace the upward, downward, and hovering patterns of a bee's flight.

- Movement can be used to show recognition of pitch *contours*.

Activities

1. Ask the children to listen as you use your voice to make sounds that slide up and down. You could use the syllable *nee* to make the sounds or another syllable of your choice.

2. Invite the children to make voice sounds that slide up and down using the syllable you used.

3. Ask the children to watch as you extend your arm in front of your body. As you move your arm up and down, the children should use their voices and make sliding sounds to approximate the motions of your arm.

4. Play "Busy Bee" and encourage the children to listen and decide if the bee's buzzing sounds suggest flying higher and lower. As they listen to the recording again, invite them to extend an arm in front of their bodies and try to show the upward, downward, and hovering motions suggested by the bee's buzzing sounds.

5. Provide each child with crayons or color markers and a copy of the picture "Busy Bee." Encourage them to color their bee and to make it as attractive as possible. They could later cut out the bee and glue it to heavier paper.

6. Play "Busy Bee" again and invite the children to fly their bees up and down about the room in response to the upward, downward, and hovering motions suggested by the buzzing sounds in the recording.

7. For another playing of "Busy Bee," suggest to the children that they become bees and create a bee dance by flying about the room up and down and stopping occasionally to hover over a plant.

Materials and Equipment

- CD player

- recording of No. 37, "Busy Bee"

- crayons or color markers

- scissors, glue sticks, heavy bond paper

- copy of "Busy Bee" (see black line master on page 107) for each child

Related National Standards

PreK   Content Standard 1, Achievement Standard 1a
         Content Standard 2, Achievement Standard 2a
         Content Standard 3, Achievement Standard 3b, 3c
         Content Standard 4, Achievement Standard 4b

K–4   Content Standard 3, Achievement Standard 3d
         Content Standard 6, Achievement Standard 6c, 6e

Little Penguin and Great Big Polar Bear

The children listen and move creatively to music that suggests small and large animals.

The Music  Track 38

Little Penguin and Great Big Polar Bear (2:17 minutes). Two quick signal sounds are heard. These are followed by a section of music that has shorter, bouncy, happy, rhythmic, faster, higher-pitched sounds. The next section includes longer, slower, lower-pitched, mysterious sounds. The two sections are then repeated; they suggest a form of ABAB (penguin, polar bear, penguin, polar bear).

Musical Understanding Focus

Guide the children to focus on the following understandings as they listen to "Little Penguin and Great Big Polar Bear."

- Music may include shorter and longer sounds (*duration*).

- Music may include higher- and lower-pitched sounds (*pitch*).

- Music may include faster and slower sounds (*tempo*).

- Music may include *sections* that contrast with each other (ABAB *form*).

Activities

1. Invite several children to take turns showing how a little penguin might walk and do a happy dance. They should do their best to look like penguins as they dance. Then invite several other children to take turns showing how a great big polar bear might do a slow dance. Show pictures of a penguin and a polar bear if needed.

2. Divide the children into two groups: penguins and polar bears. Point to one group and ask them to do a dance that represents their animal, and then point to the other group. Give both groups an opportunity to be little penguins and great big polar bears.

3. Play the recording "Little Penguin and Great Big Polar Bear." Ask the children to listen for music they think suggests a little penguin and a great big polar bear.

4. In two groups (penguins and polar bears), have the children move to the music that seems to fit a little penguin and a great big polar bear. Cue the children only if necessary.

5. Ask the children to describe how the music for a little penguin and the music for a great big polar bear were different. Guide them to recognize such things as: penguin—faster, shorter, higher-pitched, bouncy, playful, happy sounds; polar bear—slower, plodding, longer, lower-pitched, mysterious sounds.

6. As you play "Little Penguin and Great Big Polar Bear" again, invite the children to be whatever they want to be and to create their own dance for the entire recording. Encourage them to dance in response to the sounds they hear. Afterward you might ask "who" they were as they danced (robot, bunny, elephant, sea lion, mouse, etc.).

Materials and Equipment

- CD player

- recording of No. 38, "Little Penguin and Great Big Polar Bear"

- pictures of penguin and polar bear (optional)

Related National Standards

PreK Content Standard 3, Achievement Standard 3b, 3c
Content Standard 4, Achievement Standard 4a, 4b

K–4 Content Standard 6, Achievement Standard 6a, 6b, 6d, 6e

A Jingle Bells Celebration

The children move creatively to represent variations and changes in tempo and style of a familiar melody.

The Music  Track 39

A Jingle Bells Celebration (2:19 minutes). Three high-pitched sounds signal the music will begin; the traditional jingle bells melody is presented; then nontraditional variations and rhythms based on the jingle bells melody are presented with changes in tempo and rhythm, including waltz- and march-like styles.

Musical Understanding Focus

Guide the children to focus on the following understandings as they listen to "A Jingle Bells Celebration."

- A familiar melody may sometimes be altered and presented with variations.

- A familiar melody may sometimes be presented in both march- and waltz-like styles.

- An *accompaniment* serves as a background to music intended to be in the foreground.

- Movement can be used to show recognition of contrasting rhythms and styles of a melody.

Activities

1. Invite the children to join you in singing "Jingle Bells."
2. Ask the children to sing "Jingle Bells" with you again while moving in some way to represent the happy style of the music.
3. Give a group of children simple instruments to play as all others sing the song while moving. Remind the instrument players that they are an accompaniment and should play their instruments at a loudness level that serves as a background to the singers.
4. Play "A Jingle Bells Celebration" and invite the children to move as they listen to the music.
5. As they listen to "A Jingle Bells Celebration" again, have one group of children play instruments as an accompaniment, and have another group use props and move while singing.

6. For another playing of the recording, invite all the children to choose if they want to move without using an instrument or prop, move while using a prop, or move while playing an instrument. Guide them to have a happy celebration!

Materials and Equipment

- CD player

- recording of No. 39, "A Jingle Bells Celebration"

- jingle clogs, wrist bells, jingle bells, tambourines

- scarves, 3-foot strips of colorful crepe paper, 8-inch dowels with 2-inch-long ribbons connected to one end, crepe paper pom-poms, other items

Related National Standards

PreK Content Standard 1, Achievement Standard 1a, 1c, 1d
Content Standard 2, Achievement Standard 2b
Content Standard 3, Achievement Standard 3b, 3c
Content Standard 4, Achievement Standard 4b

K–4 Content Standard 1, Achievement Standard 1a, 1b, 1c
Content Standard 2, Achievement Standard 2a, 2b, 2c
Content Standard 6, Achievement Standard 6a, 6b, 6e

Listening, Running, and Freezing

The children move creatively to show recognition of music that begins, stops, and begins again.

The Music  Track 40

Listening, Running, and Freezing (1:45 minutes). Three high-pitched sounds signal the music will begin; running music that starts on a very high pitch and then descends is heard and continues throughout the recording; the music sometimes stops abruptly, suggesting moments of freezing in position until the music starts again.

Musical Understanding Focus

Guide the children to focus on the following understandings as they listen to "Listening, Running, and Freezing."

- Music may sometimes include brief moments of silence.

- Music can have a steady *tempo* and not become faster or slower.

- Movement can be used to show recognition of when music stops and starts again.

Activities

1. With the children seated, ask them to listen as you make shaking sounds with a tambourine. They should either shake their hands fast or move their feet up and down rapidly as you shake the tambourine, and freeze in position when you stop shaking it.

2. Ask the children to stand and to run rapidly in place. Then use tambourine shaking sounds to signal when they should run in place and when they should freeze in position.

3. As you shake the tambourine again, have the children run about the area, but taking very small running steps as suggested by the music. Again, alternate between tambourine shaking sounds and brief periods of silence for freezing.

4. Play "Listening, Running, and Freezing" and invite the children to listen carefully and to run and freeze in place in response to the music.

5. As they listen to the recording again, ask them to make up their own listening, running, and freezing dance, but to create interesting and unusual freezing positions each time the music stops. You may want to have one group do this first and then the other group. This will permit the children to enjoy the freezing poses of the other children.

Materials and Equipment

- CD player

- recording of No. 40, "Listening, Running, and Freezing"

- tambourine

Related National Standards

PreK Content Standard 3, Achievement Standard 3b, 3c
Content Standard 4, Achievement Standard 4b

K–4 Content Standard 6, Achievement Standard 6c, 6e

Scarf Dance

The children use creative movement and scarves to show recognition of a flowing style of music.

The Music  Track 41

Scarf Dance (2:18 minutes). Two high-pitched signal sounds are heard. The beautiful, graceful, and flowing music is continuous and does not change in style or tempo throughout; it suggests a feeling of calm and floating in space.

Musical Understanding Focus

Guide the children to focus on the following understandings as they listen to "Scarf Dance."

- Styles of music can suggest certain kinds of emotions and feelings.

- Movement can be used to represent graceful and flowing styles of music.

- A prop can become an extension of body movement to represent a style of music.

Activities

1. Ask the children to stand and briefly march in place, making heavy stepping sounds.

2. Model for the children how to pat their thighs or tap a tabletop loudly to a steady beat. Have them follow your cues for when to pat or tap louder and softer.

3. Play "Scarf Dance" and invite the children to create their own dance for the music.

4. Afterward, ask them if they think marching with heavy steps would go well with the music of "Scarf Dance," and ask why or why not. Also ask if the rhythm patted on their thighs or tapped on a tabletop would go well with the music, and ask why or why not.

5. Provide scarves for the children to use as a prop to create a dance. You might first hold a scarf high above your head and release it so they can watch how it floats to the floor. Then let the children experiment with releasing the scarves and watching them float to the floor.

6. Provide scarves for the children to use as extensions of their bodies as they create a dance for another playing of "Scarf Dance." Encourage them to experiment with different ways to use the scarves that fit with the style of the music as they move and listen again to the recording.

Materials and Equipment

- CD player

- recording of No. 41, "Scarf Dance"

- inexpensive nylon scarves (or strips of tissue or crepe paper)

Related National Standards

PreK   Content Standard 3, Achievement Standard 3b, 3c
Content Standard 4, Achievement Standard 4a, 4b

K–4   Content Standard 6, Achievement Standard 6c, 6e

Walkers and Tiptoers

The children move creatively to the beat to show recognition of contrasting and recurring sections of music.

The Music Track 42

Walkers and Tiptoers (1:55 minutes). The music begins with low-pitched, slow, walking music; then higher-pitched tiptoe music is heard; the walking music returns; the tiptoe music returns; then walking music and tiptoe music are heard together.

Musical Understanding Focus

Guide the children to focus on the following understandings as they listen to "Walkers and Tiptoers."

- Music can suggest different ways and *tempos* to walk.

- *Sections* of music may sound different: A—walking, B—tiptoeing, A—walking, B—tiptoeing, A and B—walking and tiptoeing together (*contrast*)

- Sections of music may return after contrasting sections of music are heard (*recurrence*).

- Sections of music may create a musical *form* (ABAB, A and B together).

- Movement can be used to show recognition of contrasting and recurring sections of music.

Activities

1. Tap a moderately slow, walking beat and ask several children to walk in time with the beat.

2. Tap a faster beat and ask several children to tiptoe to the beat of the taps.

3. Play "Walkers and Tiptoers" and ask the children to listen and use their fingers on their tabletops to walk in time with the beat of the music. Guide them to recognize the sequence of musical events: walk, tiptoe, walk, tiptoe, walk and tiptoe together.

4. Divide the children into two groups: walkers and tiptoers. Play "Walkers and Tiptoers" and encourage them to listen to the music to determine when to walk and tiptoe. Especially watch to see if both groups move to the final section when both walking and tiptoeing music are included.

5. Invite the children to make up a dance as they listen to the music again. They are each to walk or tiptoe to the first four sections and then decide how they will move to the last section.

6. As they listen to "Walkers and Tiptoers" again, encourage them to create a different dance that includes funny ways to walk and tiptoe.

Materials and Equipment

- CD player

- recording of No. 42, "Walkers and Tiptoers"

Related National Standards

PreK Content Standard 3, Achievement Standard 3b, 3c
Content Standard 4, Achievement Standard 4b

K–4 Content Standard 3, Achievement Standard 3b
Content Standard 6, Achievement Standard 6a, 6b, 6c, 6e

Funny Halloween Creatures

The children move creatively to portray imaginary creatures suggested by the sounds of music.

The Music  Track 43

Funny Halloween Creatures (2:11 minutes). Three tapping sounds, heard twice, signal that the music will begin; the music consists of random voice and instrumental sounds against a rhythmic background to portray any kind of funny, peculiar, Halloween creature one might imagine.

Musical Understanding Focus

Guide the children to focus on the following understandings as they listen to "Funny Halloween Creatures."

- Musical sounds can suggest imaginary characters and events.
- Music can include funny, weird, mysterious voice and instrumental sounds.

- Movement can be used to portray imaginary creatures suggested by the sounds in music.

- Unusual creative movements can be used in time with the *beat* of music.

- An *accompaniment* should serve as a background to the music intended to be in the foreground.

Activities

1. Ask the children if they have seen funny masks worn by children during Halloween. Let them take turns describing what they have seen. Focus the discussion on the idea of "funny" rather than "scary."

2. Provide materials for the children to create funny Halloween creature masks they can wear.

3. When the masks are completed, have them listen to "Funny Halloween Creatures." Encourage them to think about what kind of dance they might do to the beat and funny sounds of the music.

4. Invite them to wear their masks as they listen and move to "Funny Halloween Creatures" and create a dance for the creatures their masks portray.

5. Play "Funny Halloween Creatures" again and ask the children to remain seated and to create a background (an accompaniment) of funny voice sounds to go with the music—but at a loudness level that will permit the recorded music to be in the foreground.

6. For other playings of "Funny Halloween Creatures," invite the children in small groups to wear their masks, make accompaniment sounds, and create another dance to the music.

Materials and Equipment

- CD player

- recording of No. 43, "Funny Halloween Creatures"

- materials for making paper masks (paper, color markers, string, scissors, staples, etc.)

Related National Standards

PreK Content Standard 1, Achievement Standard 1a
Content Standard 2, Achievement Standard 2c
Content Standard 3, Achievement Standard 3b, 3c
Content Standard 4, Achievement Standard 4b

K–4 Content Standard 3, Achievement Standard 3a
Content Standard 6, Achievement Standard 6b, 6e

Old MacDonald's Animals

The children listen, sing, and move creatively to show recognition of sections in music.

The Music  Track 44

Old MacDonald's Animals (1:47 minutes). Three short signal sounds are heard; these are followed by the first verse, where children could join in and sing "… and on this farm he had a horse, and the horse it walked this way"; then horse and walking sounds are heard; second verse "… and on this farm he had some chickens, and the chickens they walked this way," then chicken and walking sounds are heard; third verse "… and on this farm he had a cow, and the cow it walked this way," cow and walking sounds are heard; ending section.

Musical Understanding Focus

Guide the children to focus on the following understandings as they listen to "Old MacDonald's Animals."

- Verses of songs usually have the same *melody*.

- Listeners who become familiar with a musical selection can learn when to join in and sing and move.

- Movement can be used to show recognition of *sections* and different *timbres* of music.

Activities

1. Ask the children to join you in singing the song "Old MacDonald." Then ask them to name some of the animals Old MacDonald had on his farm. Encourage them to name as many farm animals as they can.

2. Invite the children to take turns naming an animal and then imitating the sounds the animal might make and the way it walks (ducks, turkeys, cats, dogs, cows, goats, horses, etc.).

3. Invite the children to take turns imitating the sounds of flying birds that might visit Old MacDonald's farm (owls, crows, geese, mocking birds, etc.).

4. Teach the children to sing these three verses:

    v.1 Old MacDonald had a horse, and the horse it walked this way.

    v.2 Old MacDonald had some chickens, and the chickens they walked this way.

    v.3 Old MacDonald had a cow, and the cow it walked this way.

5. Play "Old MacDonald's Animals" and help the children join in singing the verses after the introduction sections are heard. Especially ask them to listen to the animal sounds and their walking sounds between each verse.

6. Play "Old MacDonald's Animals" and invite small groups of children (horses, chickens, cows) to walk creatively to the music that occurs right after each verse. All other children could participate as singers.

7. Play "Old MacDonald's Animals" and invite all children to make up their own dance to the music.

Materials and Equipment

- CD player

- recording of No. 44, "Old MacDonald's Animals"

Related National Standards

PreK Content Standard 1, Achievement Standard 1a, 1b
Content Standard 3, Achievement Standard 3a, 3b, 3c
Content Standard 4, Achievement Standard 4b

K–4 Content Standard 1, Achievement Standard 1c
Content Standard 6, Achievement Standard 6a, 6b, 6d, 6e

The Blues Movers

The children move creatively to show recognition of different instrumental timbres and the steady beat of music.

The Music  Track 45

The Blues Movers (2:06 minutes). The music begins with a drum-set introduction; then four different sounds improvise music to the background of a 12-bar blues chord progression (each instrument improvises for 12 measures) with brief drum-set interludes separating each improvisation. The order of events is drum-set introduction, trombone-like improvisation, drum-set interlude, flute-like improvisation, drum-set interlude, trumpet-like improvisation, drum-set interlude, clarinet-like improvisation.

Musical Understanding Focus

Guide the children to focus on the following understandings as they listen to "The Blues Movers."

- Music sometimes has a steady *beat* throughout.

- Musical instruments have different *timbres* (tone qualities).

- Music can be improvised (made up while playing).

- Rhythms can be improvised and played as a background of sound to recorded music.

- Movement can be used to show recognition of different instrumental timbres.

Activities

1. Play "The Blues Movers" and invite the children to create their own dance as they listen and move to the music.

2. Afterward, ask them to describe what they heard. You might ask questions like these to help them reflect on what they heard. Ask, "Did the music become faster or slower, or did it stay the same throughout?" "Was one instrument or were several instruments featured in the music?" "Did the music sound sad, scary, funny, bouncy?" "What words can you use to describe it?"

3. Divide the children into four groups: trombone, flute, trumpet, clarinet. As they listen to "The Blues Movers" again, each group is to create a dance for the instrument they represent. Cue the groups when to begin and when to stop moving only if necessary.

4. For other playings of "The Blues Movers," you could have the children in small groups use rhythm instruments such as jingle clogs, rhythm sticks, tambourines, and maracas to improvise rhythms to the beat of the music. Remind them to play their instruments at a loudness level that will serve as a background to the music (*accompaniment*).

5. Play "The Blues Movers" again and invite all the children to create a dance that will show their recognition of the beat of the music.

Materials and Equipment

- CD player

- recording of No. 45, "The Blues Movers"

- rhythm instruments such as jingle clogs, rhythm sticks, tambourines, and maracas

Related National Standards

PreK   Content Standard 1, Achievement Standard 1d
Content Standard 3, Achievement Standard 3a, 3b, 3c
Content Standard 4, Achievement Standard 4b

K–4   Content Standard 2, Achievement 2b
Content Standard 6, Achievement Standard 6a, 6b, 6d, 6e

Marching with the Saints

The children use movement to show recognition of different instrumental timbres and changes in tempo.

The Music  Track 46

Marching with the Saints (2:06 minutes). Four drum-like sounds signal the music is to begin; then an introduction by percussion-like sounds is presented; clarinet-like sounds play the melody: then a slower, slippery trombone-like sound plays it; then a muted trumpet-like sound plays the melody faster; and finally a slow, tuba-like sound plays the melody and ends on a very low-pitched note.

Musical Understanding Focus

Guide the children to focus on the following understandings as they listen to "Marching with the Saints."

- A melody can be presented in many different ways.

- Musical instruments can be recognized and identified by their *timbres* (tone qualities).

- Music can be fast, slow, and slow down gradually (*ritardando*).

- Movement can be used to show recognition of different instrumental timbres and *tempo* changes.

Activities

1. Sing with the children "When the Saints Go Marching In" or another song they know. You could have them clap the beat as they sing.

2. Have the children sing the song again in the following ways to create different timbres (qualities of sound).

   - Sing the song fast. Sing the song slow.

   - Begin singing the song fast and gradually slow down.

   - Sing the song without moving the lips.

   - Sing the song while holding their noses closed.

3. Invite the children to suggest other ways to sing the song that will create different kinds of timbres. Try out their suggestions.

4. Play "Marching with the Saints" and ask the children to listen for the different kinds of sounds that play the melody.

5. Divide the children into four groups. Each group is to move to the music when the four different sounds play the melody. Cue the children when to begin or stop moving only if necessary.

   - *Group 1*   clarinet   - *Group 3*   violin

   - *Group 2*   trombone   - *Group 4*   tuba

6. Invite all the children or small groups of children to create their own dance for the entire recording of "Marching with the Saints." Encourage them to try out funny movements when the music sounds funny.

Materials and Equipment

- CD player

- recording of No. 46, "Marching with the Saints"

Related National Standards

PreK   Content Standard 1, Achievement Standard 1a, 1b
           Content Standard 3, Achievement Standard 3b, 3c
           Content Standard 4, Achievement Standard 4b

K–4   Content Standard 1, Achievement Standard 1a, 1b
           Content Standard 6, Achievement Standard 6a, 6b, 6d, 6e

Pan-popped Popcorn

The children move creatively to illustrate recognition of examples of *accelerando* and *ritardando*.

The Music  Track 47

Pan-popped Popcorn (1:33 minutes). Three popping signal sounds are heard; popcorn is poured into a pan; popping sounds are heard first slowly, then gradually faster and faster; the pops then become less frequent as the popping process ends.

Musical Understanding Focus

Guide the children to focus on the following understandings as they listen to "Pan-popped Popcorn."

- Sounds that begin slowly and gradually become faster are an example of *accelerando*.

- Sounds that are fast and gradually become slower are an example of *ritardando*.

- Movement can be used to illustrate examples of *accelerando* and *ritardando*.

Activities

1. Ask the children to hold their hands chest high in front of them and to slowly shake their hands. Then ask them to shake their hands fast.

2. Play a game to illustrate *accelerando*. They should shake their hands on your verbal cues such as: "shake your hands very slow, a little faster, faster yet, real fast."

3. Play a similar game to illustrate *ritardando* using cues such as: "real fast, a little slower, very slow."

4. Ask the children to describe what happens when they hear popcorn popping in a pan (kernels pop slowly at first, then faster, then less frequently).

5. Play "Pan-popped Popcorn" and invite the children to shake their hands to illustrate what they hear.

6. Invite the children to create their own dance as they listen again to "Pan-popped Popcorn." You could later ask them to illustrate kernels in a pan getting hotter, wiggling fast, then "pop," and then to strike a popped kernel pose. Let them enjoy each other's popped kernel poses.

Materials and Equipment

- CD player

- recording of No. 47, "Pan-popped Popcorn"

Related National Standards

PreK Content Standard 3, Achievement Standard 3a, 3b, 3c
Content Standard 4, Achievement Standard 4b

K–4 Content Standard 6, Achievement Standard 6a, 6b, 6c, 6d, 6e

Index

Music Concepts and Aspects Highlighted in the Activities

Busy Bee

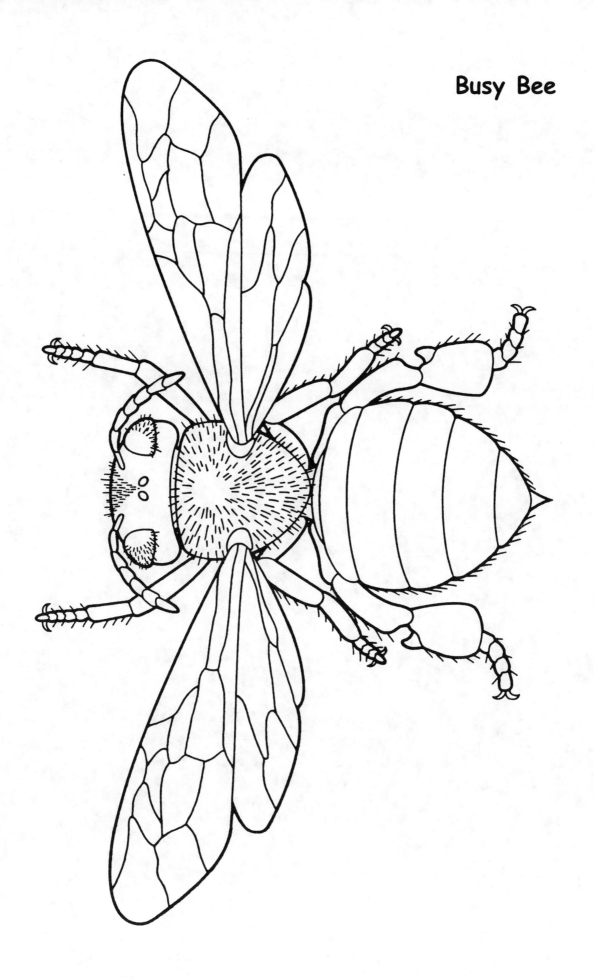

MENC Prekindergarten Standards for Music Education

1. CONTENT STANDARD: Singing and playing instruments
Achievement Standards:
Children

    a. use their voices expressively as they speak, chant, and sing
    b. sing a variety of simple songs in various keys, meters, and genres (e.g., folk songs, ethnic songs, singing games), alone and with a group, becoming increasingly accurate in rhythm and pitch
    c. experiment with a variety of instruments and other sound sources
    d. play simple melodies and accompaniments on instruments

2. CONTENT STANDARD: Creating music

Achievement Standards:
Children

    a. improvise songs to accompany their play activities
    b. improvise instrumental accompaniments to songs, recorded selections, stories, and poems
    c. create short pieces of music, using voices, instruments, and other sound sources
    d. invent and use original graphic or symbolic systems to represent vocal and instrumental sounds and musical ideas

3. CONTENT STANDARD: Responding to music

Achievement Standards:
Children

    a. identify the sources of a wide variety of sounds (e.g., crying baby, piano, guitar, car horn, bursting balloon)
    b. respond through movement to music of various tempos, meters, dynamics, modes, genres, and styles to express what they hear and feel in works of music
    c. participate freely in music activities

4. CONTENT STANDARD: Understanding music

Achievement Standards:
Children

    a. use their own vocabulary and standard music vocabulary to describe voices, instruments, music notation, and music of various genres, styles, and periods from diverse cultures
    b. sing, play instruments, move, or verbalize to demonstrate awareness of the elements of music and changes in their usage (e.g., changes in rhythm, dynamics, tempo)
    c. demonstrate an awareness of music as a part of daily life

K–4 National Standards for Music Education

1. CONTENT STANDARD: Singing, alone and with others, a varied repertoire of music

Achievement Standards:

Students

    a. sing independently, on pitch and in rhythm, with appropriate timbre, diction, and posture, and maintain a steady tempo

    b. sing expressively, with appropriate dynamics, phrasing, and interpretation

    c. sing from memory a varied repertoire of songs representing genres and styles from diverse cultures

    d. sing ostinatos, partner songs, and rounds

    e. sing in groups, blending vocal timbres, matching dynamic levels, and responding to the cues of a conductor

2. CONTENT STANDARD: Performing on instruments, alone and with others, a varied repertoire of music

Achievement Standards:

Students

    a. perform on pitch, in rhythm, with appropriate dynamics and timbre, and maintain a steady tempo

    b. perform easy rhythmic, melodic, and chordal patterns accurately and independently on rhythmic, melodic, and harmonic classroom instruments

    c. perform expressively a varied repertoire of music representing diverse genres and styles

    d. echo short rhythms and melodic patterns

    e. perform in groups, blending instrumental timbres, matching dynamic levels, and responding to the cues of a conductor

    f. perform independent instrumental parts while other students sing or play contrasting parts

3. CONTENT STANDARD: Improvising melodies, variations, and accompaniments

Achievement Standards:

Students

    a. improvise "answers" in the same style to given rhythmic and melodic phrases

    b. improvise simple rhythmic and melodic ostinato accompaniments

    c. improvise simple rhythmic variations and simple melodic embellishments on familiar melodies

    d. improvise short songs and instrumental pieces, using a variety of sound sources, including traditional sounds, nontraditional sounds available in the classroom, body sounds, and sounds produced by electronic means

4. CONTENT STANDARD: Composing and arranging music within specified guidelines

Achievement Standards:

Students

    a. create and arrange music to accompany readings or dramatizations

    b. create and arrange short songs and instrumental pieces within specified guidelines

    c. use a variety of sound sources when composing

5. CONTENT STANDARD: Reading and notating music

Achievement Standards:

Students

    a. read whole, half, dotted half, quarter, and eighth notes and rests in 2/4, 3/4, and 4/4 meter signatures

    b. use a system (that is, syllables, numbers, or letters) to read simple pitch notation in the treble clef in major keys

    c. identify symbols and traditional terms referring to dynamics, tempo, and articulation and interpret them correctly when performing

    d. use standard symbols to notate meter, rhythm, pitch, and dynamics in simple patterns presented by the teacher

6. CONTENT STANDARD: Listening to, analyzing, and describing music

Achievement Standards:

Students

    a. identify simple music forms when presented aurally

    b. demonstrate perceptual skills by moving, by answering questions about, and by describing aural examples of music of various styles representing diverse cultures

    c. use appropriate terminology in explaining music, music notation, music instruments and voices, and music performances

    d. identify the sounds of a variety of instruments, including many orchestra and band instruments, and instruments from various cultures, as well as children's voices and male and female adult voices

    e. respond through purposeful movement to selected prominent music characteristics or to specific music events while listening to music

7. CONTENT STANDARD: Evaluating music and music performances

Achievement Standard:

Students

    a. devise criteria for evaluating performances and compositions

    b. explain, using appropriate music terminology, their personal preferences for specific musical works and styles

8. CONTENT STANDARD: Understanding relationships between music, the other arts, and disciplines outside the arts

Achievement Standards:

Students

    a. identify similarities and differences in the meanings of common terms used in the various arts

b. identify ways in which the principles and subject matter of other disciplines taught in the school are interrelated with those of music

9. CONTENT STANDARD: Understanding music in relation to history and culture

Achievement Standards:

Students

    a. identify by genre or style aural examples of music from various historical periods and cultures

    b. describe in simple terms how elements of music are used in music examples from various cultures of the world

    c. identify various uses of music in their daily experiences and describe characteristics that make certain music suitable for each use

    d. identify and describe roles of musicians in various music settings and cultures

    e. demonstrate audience behavior appropriate for the context and style of music performed

Children in the Photographs

Bronte Amoy

Bethany Baker

Celine Casamina

Brandee-gail Chun

Kuk'a Derouin

Peter Fee

Carla Gouveia

Jenifer Hu

Devin Jandoc

Camerone Kajioka

Cassandra Lesa

Preston Muronaga

Thomas Parpana IV

Madison Peacock

Lensa Reynold

Salam Sarameh

Reyn Sugai

Ryan Tokunaga

Charna Underwood

John "Keola" Vertido

Joshua Vittitow

Jessica Warner

Piper Whalen

Selected MENC Early Childhood Publications

Strategies for Teaching Prekindergarten Music. Provides seventy practical strategies that help children sing and play instruments, create music, respond to music, and understand music. Contains step-by-step instructions for each strategy. Compiled and edited by Wendy L. Sims. 1995. 96 pages. Stock #1644.

Strategies for Teaching K-4 General Music. Provides thirty-six strategies that reflect a variety of teaching and learning styles. Contains step-by-step instructions for each strategy. Compiled and edited by Sandra L. Stauffer and Jennifer Davidson. 1996. 72 pages. Stock #1645.

Prekindergarten Music Education Standards (brochure). Contains content and achievement standards for children aged 2–4; standards specifying the necessary physical and educational conditions necessary to enable every student to meet the content and achievement standards; resource list. 1995. Set of 10 brochures. Stock # 4015.

Music in Prekindergarten: Planning and Teaching. Designed to assist teachers in their efforts to help every child reach his or her full musical potential. Includes chapters on long-range goals; guidelines for music activities and instruction; music for children with special needs; developing music concepts and vocabulary; and observing, documenting, interpreting, and evaluating music behaviors. By Mary Palmer and Wendy L. Sims. 1993. 80 pages. Stock #1031.

TIPS: Music Activities in Early Childhood. Presents ideas about the most effective, developmentally appropriate, and enjoyable ways to introduce young children to music. Included are ideas for developing different musical concepts, managing groups of children, and developing community interest in early childhood music programs. Compiled by John M. Feierabend. 1990. 32 pages. Stock # 1097.

Readings in Early Childhood Music Education. A compilation of articles that present ideas on the role of music in the education and development of young children. A position statement from the National Association for the Education of Young Children on developmentally appropriate practices is included. Edited and compiled by Barbara L. Andress and Linda Miller Walker. 1992. 112 pages. Stock #1043.

Promising Practices: Prekindergarten Music Education. Identifies and describes some of the most promising early childhood education programs in the U.S. Focuses on the need for presenting age-appropriate materials in dynamic learning environments. Presents ideas for reaching children, training teachers, and evaluating instruction. Edited by Barbara Andress. 1989. 120 pages. Stock #1498.

For complete ordering information on these and other publications, write:

MENC Publications Sales
1806 Robert Fulton Drive
Reston, VA 20191-4348
Credit card holders may call 1-800-828-0229